- A 👉 in the text denotes a highly recommended sight
- A complete A–Z of practical information starts on p.109
- Extensive mapping on cover flaps and throughout text

Berlitz Publishing Company, Inc.

Princeton   Mexico City   Dublin   Eschborn   Singapore

Original Text:	Suzanne Peterson
Photography:	Erling Mandelmann
Editors:	Alan Tucker, Stephen Brewer
Layout:	Media Content Marketing, Inc.
Cartography:	GeoSystems Global Corporation
Cover Photo:	courtesy Tourism Toronto

Although we make every effort to ensure the accuracy of all information in this book, changes do occur. If you find an error in this guide, please let our editors know by writing to us at Berlitz Publishing Company, 400 Alexander Park, Princeton, NJ 08540-6306. A postcard will do.

ISBN 2-8315-6999-0
Revised 1998 — First Printing July 1998

Printed in Italy
019/807 REV

CONTENTS

Toronto

THE CITY AND ITS PEOPLE

Toronto's rise to stardom among cities is no secret. It's also nothing short of a modern miracle. Once a provincial backwater and the butt of many a derisory joke, Toronto has metamorphosed into a dynamic, vibrant metropolis of over 2 million, now the country's largest city and its centre of commerce, culture, and communications.

Visually it offers a taut contrast between glossy, contemporary buildings and older churches and houses that have been staunchly protected by conservation-minded citizens. The city's situation is itself glorious: bounded by the Don and Humber river valleys and set on a series of ravines by the expanse of Lake Ontario, it overlooks the harbour and a scattering of verdant islands.

While many people call the suburbs home, many more live in the heart of town in renovated houses or modern apartment blocks. Toronto's "neighbourhoods" are populated by a vibrant ethnic cast. Toronto reputedly has more Italian inhabitants than Florence, and there are also substantial Chinese, Hungarian, and West Indian communities. One blends into another, making an eclectic mix of cultures that offers exotic sights, sounds, and fragrances in lively profusion.

It wasn't always so. Long a humble trading post, settled by French traders in the 17th century, Toronto served briefly as capital of Upper Canada, thanks to Lieutenant-Governor John Graves Simcoe, who founded the city in 1793 and called it York, after George III's son, Frederick, Duke of York. But poor "Muddy York" never got very far as capital—especially after Americans burned down most of the settlement during the War of 1812.

York's fortunes revived as refugees from Europe settled here in the wake of the Napoleonic Wars. Finally, with incorporation in 1834, the town took back its original Indian name, Toronto, which means "meeting place." Power was in the hands of a group of Anglo-Saxon lawyers, bankers, and financiers known as the Family Compact, who also laid down rigid moral laws. Immersed in puritanical traditions, the city earned itself the epithet "Toronto the Good."

When Ottawa was designated capital of the United Province of Canada in 1855, Toronto seemed hardly to notice, and for almost a century life went on in the same staid manner. But then, shortly after World War II, a huge influx of immigrants from the four corners of the earth started to change the face and soul of the city. The St. Lawrence Seaway opened, linking Toronto to the trading nations of the world. Manufacturing industries along Lake Ontario boomed, and business flourished in the 1970s as many head offices relocated to Toronto from Montreal, in a reaction to Quebec separatism.

The 1984 opening of Toronto's multi-million-dollar Convention Centre merely set the seal on a well-known fact: Toronto held the heartbeat of the country's business—and just about everything else as well. (In fact, Toronto is now called "Hollywood North" due to the increasing number of films being shot here.) The strict "blue laws" regulating drinking and commerce on Sundays which drove everybody off the streets— sometimes all the way to Buffalo—were repealed, and weekends in Toronto became fun.

Now it's Americans who cross the border, headed for Toronto, with its cosmopolitan atmosphere and lively entertainment. The Old Guard may be pursing their lips in private, but everyone admits Toronto's new look is exciting—and good for business as well.

Toronto is the hub of Ontario—a vast province of 1,068,582 sq km (417,000 square miles), greater in area than France and Spain together. Agriculture and mining flourish, along with banking and industry, which includes everything from manufacturing cars to producing microchips. But the population density is so low that you don't have to go far to find wide-open spaces and forested lakeland—even uncharted wilderness.

In eastern Ontario, the nation's capital, Ottawa, has undergone a rejuvenation of its own and offers a wealth of natural and man-made beauties for the traveller to enjoy.

Functional and fun: Toronto's wide-open spaces on a bicycle built for two.

Many visitors to Ontario may go no farther than Niagara Falls; others plan their leisure days around the marvellous Shakespeare festival in Stratford or the Shaw Festival in Niagara-on-the-Lake, both of which are summer events.

But Toronto attracts visitors year-round, with everything a big city can offer. Activity goes on night and day. Joggers get out early, while in the evenings there are classical and rock concerts, ballet, theatre, and movies. Cabaret acts and discos round out the night scene, and there are endless fairs and festivals.

Getting around is easy—by the efficient subway (underground), by taxi, or by frequent buses, if you don't have your own car. And walking is a real pleasure, since it's both scenic and safe to walk most streets at all hours.

Eating out can be anything, from fast food or vegetarian cooking to the haughtiest of French *haute cuisine*. You can spend an evening in a raucous spaghetti parlour or German beer-hall, or in any number of ethnic restaurants.

Toronto is something of a shopper's paradise. From fashionable Bloor Street to the magnificent high-tech Eaton Centre to the harbour, thousands of shops lure the eager shopper in with tempting displays and bargains. Antiques collectors browse in the big Harbourfront markets, while other shoppers check out the countless attractive boutiques. Many of the city's shops seem to be underground in one of the new subsurface malls, a practical alternative when winter winds blow and a cool respite when summer days get too warm.

The weather extremes don't faze Ontarians, who take advantage of every season. Spring and fall offer typical North American pleasures—a pastel palette of flowers and blossoming trees in the spring, a riot of primary colours as fall changes maples and birch to flaming red or yellow against the green conifers.

If summer heat and humidity occasionally edge up to wilting levels, there is plenty of green parkland to resort to, plus Lake Ontario and some 400,000 smaller lakes to cool off in. Winter brings sub-zero temperatures, but the frozen landscape is appealing; people take to their ice skates and cross-country skis.

Toronto also offers incomparable museums, including the Royal Ontario Museum, with its large collection of Buddhist art and paleontology, and the new Gardiner Museum, which specializes in rare porcelains. Ontario Place is the delightful setting for an outdoor summer theatre, cinema, Canadian exhibits, and other less serious amusements. In the Don Valley, the spectacular Ontario Science Centre has so much to see and do that adults tend to be more reluctant to go home at the end of the day than their children are, and, in another valley farther east, the Metro Zoo houses animals from all over the world.

Meeting people is easy—in cafés, boutiques, museums. Everyone seems relaxed and open. And wherever you're from, your accent doesn't matter in this international city. Canada is officially bilingual—English and French—but English is the preferred language here, although you will hear plenty of other languages spoken.

Toronto is truly a melting pot of languages, races, and cultures. It is this cultural diversity that makes the city the exciting place that it is today.

In Toronto, you're an efficient, clean, and quiet subway ride from almost anywhere you'd want to go.

A BRIEF HISTORY

The first human beings to come to the North American continent some 50,000 years ago were nomadic peoples who crossed from northeast Asia via the Bering Strait in the wake of the last Ice Age. Over several millennia they spread southward through Mexico, dividing into clans and tribes with their own languages and cultures.

The native peoples evolved in various ways. Some lived off the bounty of the sea, others were farmers, hunters, and foragers. European explorers arrived in the 16th century.

New France

After the discoveries of Columbus, the ambitious French King Francis I (1515–1547) commissioned Giovanni da Verrazzano in 1524 to sail across the ocean and stake France's claim in the New World. Ten years later, Jacques Cartier, looking for a northwest passage to Asia, came to the Gulf of St. Lawrence. He sailed up the river to a place called Hoche Laga, which he named Mont Real (Mount Royal) for the majestic-looking hill dominating the village. In the name of France, Cartier called the lands Kannata, the Algonquin word for "settlement."

After that, French enthusiasm waned over about 75 years, until a fad for beaver hats and trim opened up new possibilities for the fur trade. But it wasn't only furs that attracted the French to Canada; they also recognized its vast, untapped mineral and timber resources, as well as its strategic value as a base in case of war with Spain. And missionaries sought to spread Christianity among the new-found heathens.

Thus in 1603 and 1604 Samuel de Champlain sailed up the St. Lawrence and Ottawa rivers to the place where Ottawa now stands. Much of the land was claimed as New

France, and in 1608 Champlain founded Quebec, which later became the first main town-settlement.

At this time, the Toronto area was inhabited by Indians. Samuel de Champlain sent his young companion Etienne Brulé there in 1615 to establish relations, which he did —living with the Indians and learning their language. It wasn't until 1750 that the site was considered important enough for a fort —little more than a storage house at that. But, as the fur trade picked up, a stronger fort, Rouillé, was built by the French to intercept Indians trading with the British across the lake.

Throughout the 17th century, the French made deep inroads into the American interior, as far as the Rocky Mountains and south to the Gulf of Mexico. They founded Detroit, St. Louis, and New Orleans, and claimed most of the Midwest. Louis Jolliet and Father Marquette were the first Europeans to see the Mississippi River.

The British were also in the colonizing business, establishing settlements along most of the American Eastern Seaboard, from Maine down to Georgia. In 1610, Henry Hudson, in the service of the Dutch East India Company, discovered the enormous bay that bears his name, and in 1670 the Hudson's Bay Company—even today an important Canadian retailing organisation—was founded by the British to promote the fur trade.

The Indians themselves had not gained much from the coming of the white man. Diseases from Europe, to which they had no immunity, ravaged the population. They were seduced by whisky and other alcoholic concoctions. And the introduction of guns and metal weapons gave fresh and deadly impetus to the feuds between the southern Iroquois tribes and the Hurons to the north. From the 1640s to the 1660s, they clashed violently, terrorizing and killing any Europeans who happened to be in the way.

The French and the British had their own battles to fight. Rivalry between the two European powers had been carried over to the New World, and the stage was being set for confrontation. In Canada, the Indians were undecided in their loyalties, but mostly they sided with the French. After vicious fighting, the British marched on Fort Frontenac in 1758, outmaneuvering the French for an easy victory. The British went on to take the fort at Niagara the following year. When the news reached the French, they burned down Fort Rouillé to keep it out of British hands.

After a protracted battle for Quebec City, on the night of September 12, 1759, General James Wolfe managed to sneak 4,500 British soldiers behind the city's defenses, surprising the French and their astute and capable leader, Louis, Marquis de Montcalm. The ensuing battle on the Plains of Abraham was brief and bloody. Both leaders perished in the fray: Wolfe survived just long enough to hear of his victory. Montcalm died of his wounds a few hours later. After a five-day siege, Quebec surrendered.

Here, the fate of the North American continent was more or less decided. Following the Treaty of Paris in 1763, the British took over administration of the territory. New France was nothing more than an idle dream, although a French presence and influence in Canada would always remain.

Americans and Loyalists

By 1775, the restive, rebellious American colonies south of Canada were seething with discontent, and the resultant revolution was to make its mark on Canada as well. Among the colonists' grievances was the Quebec Act of 1774, by which the British Parliament intended to provide French Canadians with a more suitable and fairer form of government. But the Protestants in America saw this as a dangerous concession to

Roman Catholicism. They decided to eliminate the French threat by marching on Canada.

In November 1775, the Continental Army set out under generals Richard Montgomery and Benedict Arnold—who was later convicted of treason. Montgomery's forces took Montreal, but the general was killed. Arnold's troops, facing a British-French alliance in Quebec, failed to capture the city. In 1776, more pressing matters—the American Revolution—caused the Americans to abandon their bid to take control of Canada.

During and after the Revolution, the Loyalists, American colonists who had remained loyal to the British crown, were obliged to flee to safer territory in Canada, some 7,000 of them to Ontario. Canada also attracted other ambitious Americans from south of the border, opportunists who wanted to take advantage of the grants of free land offered to Loyalists.

The Canada Act of 1791 split the colony into two provinces, Lower Canada (Quebec)—mainly populated by the original settlers, or *Canadiens*—and Upper Canada (Ontario), stronghold of the Loyalists, with its capital at Niagara-on-the-Lake. Each was headed by a lieutenant-governor.

In 1792, the Lieutenant Governor of Upper Canada, John Graves Simcoe, moved the capital from Niagara-on-the-Lake to London for strategic reasons—the former was too close to the American border. But London was also vulnerable, and finally, in 1793, Toronto was chosen as capital and renamed York.

The new capital was swampy, unattractive, and unpromising in every way. Undaunted, Simcoe encouraged construction and development, including the building of Yonge Street, which would cut right up through the province to Lake Simcoe north of the city.

The Canadians were not left long in peace by their American neighbours. British attempts to disrupt America's At-

The Loyalists

They came from every class and walk of life. Lawyers and labourers, clergymen, soldiers and farmers, craftsmen, scholars and peasants, Iroquois Indians, immigrants, and black African slaves.

Their motives ranged from the noblest to the most self-seeking. But, political or personal, the one common aim that united this extraordinary mixture of people was the defence of the United Empire.

It wasn't easy in the 13 rebel colonies for the 250,000 stalwarts who remained loyal to the Crown. Regarded as traitors, they were harassed, occasionally beaten up or tarred and feathered, and often driven out of their communities. Loyalists lost their voting rights, were unable to sell land or recover debts, and suddenly found it impossible to become lawyers, doctors, and teachers.

Then, after almost ten years of hostility and humiliation, came the bitter pill: the Treaty of Paris (1783), which acknowledged the independence of the United States. For the Loyalists who had stayed, it meant only one thing—immediate exile.

Of more than 80,000 Loyalists who fled during the period, half went to England and the British West Indies. In 1783 alone, almost 30,000 went by sea to Nova Scotia, tripling its population. Thousands of others trekked by ox cart and on foot to the St. Lawrence River and the shores of Lake Ontario.

They were far from pioneers, and ill equipped to deal with the rigors of their new life in Canada. Many died.

Six years later, Britain acknowledged the Loyalists' contribution by announcing that all those who had remained loyal were entitled to add the letters U.E. (United Empire) to their names. The privilege was extended to their families and descendants—a distinction that has often proved useful in terms of social and financial standing.

lantic trade routes led to the War of 1812, and the Americans invaded Canada while the British were busy fighting Napoleon's forces in Europe. But the Americans were relying on support from the Canadian Indians—who finally decided, with a few exceptions, to side with the British.

Still underpopulated, Upper Canada was defended by only 1,600 British soldiers led by Major-General Isaac Brock, who won some early victories, notably at Fort Michilimackinac, where Lake Huron meets Lake Michigan. The American forces attacking Montreal were demoralized and gave up without a battle. A big American thrust on the Niagara Frontier in October 1812 was finally repulsed by the British with their Indian allies, but the death of Brock during the battle was a blow to the British. Another notable leader, the Shawnee chief Tecumseh, died during the Battle of the Thames River.

In April 1813, as the war dragged on, the Americans burned and looted York and Niagara-on-the-Lake. The British retaliated with an attack on Washington in 1814 that gave the White House its final look and name: blackened by smoke, it had to be repainted white and has been that way ever since.

The war finally ran out of steam and was officially ended with the Treaty of Ghent in 1814, though skirmishes continued along the borders for years.

Growth and Consolidation

York and the rest of Canada expanded as refugees fled the Napoleonic Wars and the sweatshop conditions of the Industrial Revolution in Great Britain. In 1834, York was incorporated and took back its original Indian name, Toronto.

At this time, factions in both Upper and Lower Canada were moving toward revolt. In Lower Canada, French-speaking Canadians were agitating for government more responsible to the people. Fighting broke out in November 1837; the rebels fought several pitched battles with British troops before finally being defeated in 1838.

In Upper Canada another rebellion had been brewing—this one directed against the privileged group, known as the Family Compact, that held the reins of power. The instigator of the revolt was William Lyon Mackenzie, a fearless Scot, editor of *The Colonial Advocate* and supporter of a more broadly democratic government than that offered by the conservative ruling elite. In December 1837, Mackenzie and his followers attempted to enter Toronto to overthrow the government, but were quickly overcome; Mackenzie fled to the United States, where he remained in exile.

The British parliament took note of the discontent, appointing as governor-general Lord Durham, who recommended "anglification" as a neat solution for both Upper and

Lower Canada. In 1841, Great Britain created the united Province of Canada —comprising both main provinces—as a concession to the people's desire for more independence, and William Lyon Mackenzie was allowed to return home.

As Canada's vast resources were realized—especially Ontario's lumber

This statue in Kingston is a tribute to first prime minister Sir John A. Macdonald.

industry—new waves of immigrants poured into the region. Canals were built to transport goods and further unite the country; these included the Welland, linking Fort Erie to Niagara-on-the-Lake, and the Rideau, joining Kingston, on Lake Ontario east of Toronto, to Ottawa.

As Canada prospered, Toronto remained the centre of a wealthy Protestant elite whose strait-laced principles kept the city under a tight rein well into the 20th century.

Independence

Meanwhile, a rift was growing between Protestant English Canada and Catholic French Canada. Soon it became clear to everyone—French-Canadian, British-Canadian, and British alike—that Canada would have to have its own democratic form of government. After long negotiations, the Dominion of Canada was created on July 1, 1867, with the passing of the British North America Act in British Parliament. Upper Canada, or Canada West, became Ontario (from the Indian name for "beautiful lake") and Lower Canada, or Canada East, became Quebec.

Queen Victoria had already chosen Ottawa as a suitable capital for the united Province of Canada in 1855, partly because she'd seen an attractive watercolour of the site and partly because she thought the area would be a more neutral location than British-oriented Toronto or French-oriented Montreal.

The first prime minister was Sir John A. Macdonald, an influential architect of Canada's constitution, who envisaged a great nation stretching from ocean to ocean. The four founding provinces included Quebec, Ontario, New Brunswick, and Nova Scotia. But provision was made for others and, shortly after the turn of the century, Canada indeed reached from coast to coast.

However, power was not concentrated exclusively in a central federal government, thanks mainly to one Oliver Mowat. Born of Scottish parents in Kingston, Ontario, Mowat was elected Premier of Ontario in 1872, and for the next 24 years fought many verbal battles to win sovereign rights for the provincial parliaments. As a result, the provinces achieved a good deal of autonomy—a principle which is still working today.

Modern Times

Towards the end of the 19th century, Canada, already profiting from lumber and agriculture, started to exploit its formidable mineral potential. Oil was struck around the southern tip of Lake Huron; copper and nickel were discovered at Copper Cliff and Sudbury in 1883; and subsequently silver and gold were found. Much later—in 1948—the discovery of uranium precipitated a brand-new mining boom.

Meanwhile, travel and commerce had been enhanced by the completion in 1885 of the Canadian Pacific Railway linking the east and west coasts—a stunning feat of engineering and sheer human will-power and drive.

Toronto was usually well apart from the French-English strife that so often troubled Quebec. A concession to the French-speaking Canadians came in 1896, when Sir Wilfrid Laurier, a French Roman Catholic, was elected prime minister. He stayed in office until 1911 and as a moderate staunchly resisted any involvement of the church in state matters.

In World War I, Canada fought alongside Great Britain, although many French-Canadians objected to conscription. Following the war, further waves of immigrants arrived from all over Central and Eastern Europe.

In World War II, Canada stood firmly with the Allies, losing more than 40,000 men. Prime minister throughout the war effort was William Lyon Mackenzie King (a descendant of that famous fiery Scot).

An explosion of immigration and economic development followed the war, as the vast mineral potential was further tapped and industry drew on a pool of new talent. The stolid city of Toronto was transformed by skilled and energetic new-comers from Greece, Poland, China, Pakistan, Italy, and the West Indies.

Famous Ontarians

Ontario is proud not only of the early "movers and shakers" of industry, but of some of the great intellectual, artistic, and scientific achievements of its people.

Among the scientists, Frederick G. Banting and Charles H. Best discovered insulin, Dr. Murray Barr contributed important work on the determination of sex by cell analysis, and James Collip isolated the hormone ACTH.

Alexander Graham Bell, inventor of the telephone, moved with his family to Brantford from Scotland as a young man, and carried out many of his experiments in Ontario.

The famous Group of Seven artists forged ahead with their own dynamic ways of seeing and painting the Canadian wilderness.

Distinguished writers from Ontario include Robertson Davies, Morley Callaghan, and Margaret Atwood. In the musical world, the late Glenn Gould is still recognized as one of Bach's greatest interpreters. Maureen Forrester is a renowned contralto. And Torontonian Oscar Peterson is still exciting audiences all over the world with his well-tempered jazz piano.

The film stars hailing from Toronto include Mary Pickford (whose house is a landmark on University Avenue), as well as Raymond Massey and Jason Robards, Jr., both of whom came from distinguished Toronto families.

In 1959, Queen Elizabeth II and President Dwight D. Eisenhower jointly opened the St. Lawrence Seaway — a vast engineering *tour de force* that brought Canada and the United States into closer cooperation and made it possible for Toronto to become a major port.

In the 1970s, banking and industry turned away somewhat from troubled Montreal to Toronto, creating a new boom here. Toronto remained on the whole untouched by the British-French rivalries and separatism that had caused major national problems. It just hummed along. And so, with the focus shifting from Montreal to Toronto, shining skyscrapers shot up around Bay Street — the Wall Street of Canada — alongside quaint Victorian buildings and a rejuvenated waterfront. Some excellent urban planners, kept on their toes by the constant battle between progressives and conservationists, have contrived to keep an attractive combination of historical atmosphere along with the latest contemporary buildings.

The bright, cheerful spectacle of Toronto's Carnival draws loads of visitors and locals.

Today business is still thriving, and the ethnic mix, far from causing social tensions, adds a colourful and lively element to what has become one of the most interesting and exciting cities in Canada.

FACTS and FIGURES

Geography: Ontario is Canada's largest province after Quebec, with an area of 1,068,582 sq km (417,000 square miles). Bordered by Quebec to the east and by Manitoba to the west, Ontario has approximately 400,000 freshwater lakes and 1,094 km (680 miles) of coastline along the James and Hudson bays in the north, as well as 3,710 km (2,300 miles) along the Great Lakes and St. Lawrence Seaway. Toronto stands on an almost land-locked harbour on the northwest shore of Lake Ontario. Its larger urban area (Metro Toronto) is 620 sq km (240 square miles). Ottawa lies 490 km (295 miles) northeast of Toronto at the confluence of the Ottawa, Rideau, and Gatineau rivers.

Population: Toronto: 654,000 (urban), 2,385,000 (metropolitan); Ottawa: 323,000 (urban), 721,136 (metropolitan).

Government: Canada is a constitutional monarchy with a parliamentary system of government. Canada forms part of the British Commonwealth; the official head of state is Britain's Queen Elizabeth II, represented by a governor-general—chosen by elected representatives of the Canadian people. Head of government is the prime minister, leader of the party holding the most seats in Parliament. Parliament consists of the House of Commons, its members elected by direct suffrage, and the Senate, its members appointed by the party in power in the House.

Canada is a federal country consisting of ten provinces and two northern territories. The capital is Ottawa. All provinces elect their own legislature to govern regional matters.

Toronto is governed by a Metro Council (whose chairman is appointed by the province of Ontario), a city council, and five suburban councils.

Religion: Protestants of various denominations hold a slight majority in Ontario, but there are also a great number of Roman Catholics. Most other creeds—Muslim, Buddhist, Greek Orthodox, etc.—are represented.

WHERE TO GO

Toronto is organized on a sensible grid pattern, so it is quite easy to get around, whether by the efficient public transport, taxi, or private car. Look at a map and note the main south-north arteries: Spadina and University avenues, Bay Street ("Banking Street"), commercial Yonge Street, and Church Street. Yonge Street constitutes more or less the backbone of the city. It was constructed in 1795 as a military road leading 1,883 km (1,170 miles) north to Lake Simcoe, and now the entire street system is hinged on it. The main east-west intersections (going northward from Lake Ontario) are: Front, King, Queen, Dundas, College-Carlton, and Bloor streets.

Back to the future—the Space Age comes to the waterfront at Ontario Place.

In this guide we start the sightseeing downtown near the waterfront, and then make our way northward, with detours east and west. But you can easily choose your own tour of Toronto to fit your schedule and interests. A useful first port of call is the Metropolitan Toronto Convention and Visitors Association offices in Queen's Quay Terminal at Harbourfront. In the summertime there are information kiosks outside the Art Gallery of Ontario and the Royal Ontario Museum.

WATERFRONT AREA

A great way to get oriented is a trip up the **CN Tower,** which pierces Toronto's sky like a gigantic hypodermic needle. At 553.3 metres (1,815 feet 5 inches), it beats Chicago's Sears Tower and several other giants for the title of the world's highest free-standing structure. Built between 1973 and 1975 by Canadian National (CN), the government railroad and telecommunications firm, the tower is not only a radio and television transmission mast, but also a sure-fire tourist attraction. In 1998 the tower completed an expansion in its base which contains an overhauled visitors centre as well as new shops and restaurants.

If your stomach drops away as the outdoor plexiglass elevator rushes upward, consider that the speed of ascent is 6 metres (20 feet) per second. First stop—more than 300 metres (1,122 feet) up—is the **Sky Pod,** which has two observation decks. Up here, too, is the world's highest revolving restaurant and nightclub. From this level you can look out over the whole of Toronto, with its many ravines, parks, and neighbourhoods. To the south, you'll see the lively waterfront and harbour, dotted with sails in summer, and out to the islands. The futuristic leisure complex to the west is Ontario Place. Many of the gleaming buildings of the financial core, just northeast of the CN Tower, were designed by famous architects such as Mies van der Rohe and I. M. Pei.

Another elevator takes you up to the **Space Deck,** which at 447 metres (1,465 feet) offers distant views—they say you can see all the way to Niagara Falls and Buffalo, U.S.A., on a clear day.

From this dizzying height you can also catch a glimpse of the newest addition to Toronto's skyline, the capacious **Metro Toronto Convention Centre,** opened in 1984. It boasts the latest in convention facilities, with three main halls to host receptions of up to 12,000 people. Banquet halls, other reception rooms, and a Grand Ball Room offer more space. And of course, all are provided with the latest audiovisual equipment. Adjoining the Centre is the Crown Plaza Toronto Centre, with every possible modern amenity in sporting equipment and fast communications.

Harbourfront, at one time a swampy, rundown area, has been spruced up in recent years to serve as a recreation and cultural complex. New highrises have been built and the old warehouses dramatically renovated to house shops, cafés, a theatre, and an exhibition centre. There is also a streetcar ride and a new subway under construction. The Harbourfront Antiques Market at 222 Queen's Quay (pronounced "key" in Toronto) West offers a lively assortment of bargains, from ancient china to modern crafts.

A new attraction is the **Pier,** Toronto's waterfront museum. It is located in a historic warehouse containing maritime exhibits. You can explore a 1932 tugboat as well as rent wooden boats for a self-guided tour of the harbour.

The old **Redpath Sugar Factory,** at 95 Queen's Quay East, has been turned into a museum. You can see the machinery and equipment used for sugar production, as well as a film on the harvesting and processing of sugar.

Talented street artists at Ontario Place will draw your caricature, if you dare.

The **Toronto Islands,** facing Harbourfront, are a favourite summer respite and picnic place for Torontonians. Once a peninsular part of the Scarborough Bluffs just east of the city center, these picturesque islands were isolated by a raging storm in 1858. Today they are joined by bridges so that you can walk or cycle the length of them.

Ferry boats (no cars; you may rent bicycles on the islands) leave regularly in the summer from the docks behind the Toronto Hilton Harbour Castle at the foot of Bay Street, calling at the three main islands. **Centre Island** is the most popular, but its beach and picnic areas can be crowded. **Ward's Island** is favoured by some for its lively boardwalk. (Between Centre and Ward's islands is the exclusive Royal Canadian Yacht Club, worth a visit if you belong to an affiliated organization or have a friend who will take you there.) **Hanlan's Point,** alongside Toronto Island Airport, has a beach along the western side.

Another way to enjoy the harbour scene is to take a three-hour launch tour, one of several boat tours offered. These also provide excellent views of downtown Toronto.

West along the waterfront, you reach **Ontario Place,** a major attraction for visitors and Torontonians alike. Built on three man-made islands, this charming 39-hectare (96-acre) park is part Disneyland, part cultural centre, cleverly blended into a green waterside setting. Below a grassy knoll, the Molson amphitheatre seats up to 11,000 people for its superb outdoor classical, jazz, and pop concerts.

You can't miss the Cinesphere (IMAX theatre), the white geodesic dome that resembles a half-buried golf ball. Inside, on a curved screen six stories high, films on subjects ranging from volcanic eruptions to earth and space exploration are screened. Films change every year.

Mounted on stilts, the Atlantis Pavilions offers a banqueting room, a video show, and the Yours to Discover Theatre.

The Children's Village is beautifully and imaginatively designed for youngsters aged 4 to 14. There's a waterslide down a miniature mountain, a series of duck ponds for toddlers to splash in, a large trampoline, a children's theatre, and many other delights. And before you move on, you can put your drenched kids through the huge "dryer" shaped like a bird.

Just inland from Ontario Place, **Exhibition Place** stages the annual Canadian National Exhibition, along with other events during the year, such as the Canadian International Air Show and the Scottish World Festival Tattoo.

Toronto's maritime history is illustrated in the **Marine Museum of Upper Canada** (Exhibition Place, just west of Princes' Gate). It's located in what used to be the officers' quarters of Stanley Barracks, a military fortification dating back to 1841. Displays show economic and cultural changes brought about in certain areas by ships, as trading expanded along the St. Lawrence Basin and the waterways of central Canada.

Among the oddities are hooters, diving helmets, relics from sunken river vessels, and the bridge of a famous old lake steamer. If you're intrigued by the museum's scale-model ships, you'll also be fascinated by a tour of the *Ned Hanlan*, a full-size tugboat in dry dock outside, named after a famous oarsman.

The soldiers at old Fort York are still ready for battle, though their visitors these days are mostly tourists.

Five minutes away by foot, at the centre of Exhibition Park (just off Lakeshore Boulevard West), is **Canada's Sports Hall of Fame,** a national sports museum showing thousands of sporting aspirations and achievements in its two big galleries. Most disciplines are well represented, although the country's most popular sport—ice hockey—is conspicuous by its absence

Understandably enough, you'll find it reverently showcased in its own right in the new **Hockey Hall of Fame.** Located at Yonge and Front streets, this shrine to hockey houses the world's most comprehensive collection of hockey artefacts, displays, and memorabilia, including the entire collection of NHL trophies, most notably the coveted Stanley Cup.

On the opposite side of Gardiner Expressway stands **Old Fort York,** holding its own amid zooming traffic and railway tracks. It was once perched right on the lakeshore, but landfill has since pushed the shoreline southward. Constructed in 1793 by Lieutenant Governor Simcoe, the fort was destroyed by the retreating British in 1813, rebuilt in 1841, and restored in 1934 as a tourist attraction. You can admire some authentically furnished 19th-century

A little street music to accompany your shopping at St. Lawrence Market.

officer's quarters, a military surgery, and other historical displays, including a diorama of the Battle of York.

Going back past Harbourfront to the eastern reaches of Queen Street, you arrive at **The Beaches.** Here a lengthy boardwalk, peopled by dog-walkers and joggers, seems to stretch out to infinity along with the sandy beach. The Beaches, fashionably residential, has the expected number of colourful small restaurants and boutiques alongside attractive houses reminiscent of Nantucket. Nearby are Kew Gardens and Greenwood RaceTrack, where thoroughbred horses run and trotters and pacers prance.

THE HEART of DOWNTOWN

Bay Street—along which the banks are built like cathedrals—cuts through the heart of downtown. They may not be Chartres, but these latter-day money temples certainly merit attention.

However, some of the elderly neighbours are also distinguished and well worth visiting. **Union Station** is a grand Neo-Classical structure with limestone columns and Italian tile ceilings. Built in 1927, its echoing halls are still used as a railroad station, thanks to some militant preservationists who saved it from the wrecker's ball. The **Royal York** was Toronto's first big hotel. It has hosted royalty and still offers 1,375 rooms, as well as restaurants, nightclubs, and a large underground concourse lined with shops. At Church and King streets, the **King Edward Hotel** is another grandiose palace, with an elaborately carved atrium, crystal chandeliers, and Art Nouveau mirrors.

At Yonge and Front streets, an old, stately bank building, erected in 1855, houses the Hockey Hall of Fame (see previous page). In a more modern vein, the nearby concrete building is **Hummingbird Centre,** home to the National Ballet of Canada and the Canadian Opera Company. Next door is the equally important **St. Lawrence Centre for the Performing Arts,** specializing in Canadian drama. A block away, at Jarvis and Front streets, lies the big indoor-outdoor **St. Lawrence Market**—open Tuesdays to Saturdays, but most fun on Saturdays, when stalls display an inviting array of snack food and there are busker acts in the streets.

Nearby, **St. Lawrence Hall** is a beautiful mid-19th-century building restored to pink-and-green elegance in 1967. Used now by the National Ballet of Canada, it was once where P.T. Barnum displayed the midget, General Tom Thumb. In 1851, the year after the hall was built, Jenny Lind—affectionately known as the Swedish nightingale—sang here and enchanted audiences. It subsequently became an integral part of the city's social and business life. It gradually fell out of favour and into disrepair, until its comparatively recent renovation. It is now one of Toronto's finest old buildings.

Of the many striking contemporary financial buildings, you shouldn't miss the **Royal Bank Plaza,** a glimmering gold mass at the corner of Front and Bay streets that reflects much of the surrounding architecture as well. This creation of Toronto architect Boris Zerafa is covered in 2,500 ounces of real gold. Walk inside, and you'll see a cathedral-high lobby and atrium decorated with some thousands of aluminium cylinders, the work of Venezuelan sculptor Jesús Raphael Soto. Natural light shines in on the ponds, waterfall, and lush greenery, making the entire experience sparkle.

Just to the north, the **Toronto-Dominion Centre,** designed by Mies van der Rohe, is a handsome complex of black glass buildings. The 36-floor IBM Tower, which is the third-highest of the four towers, also contains a gallery of Inuit art.

In the next block north is Canada's tallest office building, **First Canadian Place.** One tower is home to the Bank of Montreal, with access through a pleasant green courtyard, complete with waterfall. The second tower houses the new **Toronto Stock Exchange,** opened in 1983. Behind the Exchange Tower there is a trading pavilion where visitors can observe the frenetic trading from an observation deck. Best hours are between 10:00 A.M. and 2:00 P.M. Besides admiring a magnificent Art-Deco setting with monumental art works in the Exchange lobby, you can also pick up audiovisual information about how stock markets work — if not the latest hot tips.

The fresh fruit available at St. Lawrence Market is a feast for the senses.

Most of the main buildings in the area are linked by a veritable labyrinth of underground concourses, including shopping malls, movie theatres, and restaurants, a boon when bad weather strikes.

No matter how it's earned, money speaks in Toronto. Two blocks west of the Stock Exchange, on King Street West, is Mirvish territory, part of the empire of Ed Mirvish, the famed tycoon who came from Lithuania and made his riches from discount retailing. Mirvish, who renovated London's Old Vic, earlier restored Toronto's Edwardian **Royal Alexandra Theatre,** and today its exuberant Broadway musicals and other productions play to packed houses. Close by is the **Princess of Wales Theatre,** constructed in the mid-1990s.

Church Street has been aptly named for its several churches: the Anglican St. James Cathedral, the United Church's Metropolitan Church, and the Roman Catholic St. Michael's Cathedral. All are worth a visit for their façades and interiors, in turn-of-the-century style.

On Bond Street, just south of Dundas, the Victorian **Mackenzie House** provides historical interest, with guides in traditional colonial dress. The first Mayor of Toronto, William Lyon Mackenzie was exiled after leading a revolt in 1837 (see page 18), but he returned later to Toronto and lived in this house until his death in 1861. The interior has been impeccably restored; you can see exhibits of Mackenzie's life and the hand-operated flatbed printing press on which he turned out his revolutionary newspaper, *The Colonial Advocate.*

An absolute imperative in Toronto is the **Eaton Centre.** Much more than just a shopping mall, it's a dazzling, grandiose complex of galleries under an arched glass roof, full of greenery, and even boasting a flock of floating fibreglass geese. A redevelopment project next to the Centre is transforming the area into a planned Times Square or Piccadilly Circus.

With such an atmosphere of super-sell, it's all the more startling to look out on the quiet form of **Holy Trinity Church,** huddled in the shadow of the Space-Age shopping complex. As one of the city's oldest buildings (1847), the church—together with its neighbour, Scadding House, formerly the home of a Toronto churchman—was accorded the dubious privilege of being allowed to remain while the concrete-and-glass Centre sprouted up around them. Holy Trinity Church's twin towers seem almost to have shrunk since the far-off days when they were imposing landmarks for sailors navigating Lake Ontario.

From the Dundas Street entry you can walk through the Eaton Centre on any level, above or below ground, all the way to Queen Street. It's about a 12-minute hike if you put on blinders and don't stop to window shop or have a snack—a near-impossible feat, since everything in these hundreds of shops beckons you to stop. Built in 1975, Eaton Centre is a monument to the merchandising family that for more than a century has followed the motto, "Goods Satisfactory or Money Refunded." A walkway over Queen Street brings you to another large department store, The Bay.

On the northeast corner of Queen Street West and Bay

Working Torontonians take a break for lunch under the trees.

stands **Old City Hall.** Now used to house Provincial Courts, it's a typical Victorian building with a large clock tower, a favourite landmark for Torontonians. Set back on Nathan Phillips Square you'll see the **New City Hall,** designed by Finnish architect Viljo Revell. Completed in 1965, it's a handsome structure with two curved towers flanking a low circular building, reminding many people of an oyster opening on its pearl. Henry Moore's statue of *The Archer* outside attracts some attention. West of the square, **Osgoode Hall** stands out as a lovely golden stone-and-brick Georgian building. Since 1832 it has been the seat of the Law Society of Upper Canada.

Campbell House, on the northwest corner of Queen and University streets, is an exemplary Georgian mansion in red brick that once belonged to Sir William Campbell, Chief Justice of Upper Canada (1825–1829). You will be shown around by guides in Colonial Dames' costumes. In 1972, the building was moved here lock, stock, and barrel from its original site about 3 km (2 miles) away.

Northwest of here, on Dundas Street around Grange Park, the **Art Gallery of Ontario,** is a highlight for art lovers (see page 46). Adjoining the gallery is **The Grange,** an elegant Georgian country house built in 1817 by d'Arcy Boulton, Jr., on property that once stretched 3½ km (2 miles) from Queen up to Bloor Street. Later, an American professor lived in the house; his widow willed it to the Art Gallery.

The house is a microcosm of fashionable life in Toronto as it was early last century. In 1973 it was restored to its former colour and grace as a typical gentleman's residence of the time. Note the circular cantilevered staircase, stained-glass windows, and statuary. What your imagination doesn't furnish, a slide presentation will—with deferential costumed staff carrying out the duties of a century and a half ago.

DOWNTOWN TORONTO

The poet Matthew Arnold, describing a visit he had made to The Grange, wrote that in all his travels he had experienced "nothing so pleasant and so home-like."

On McCaul Street, across from the Art Gallery, the **Village by the Grange** has a tempting array of boutiques and restaurants in an Old-World atmosphere.

As you go fArther west, the ambience becomes progressively Asian. Toronto's **Chinatown** originally grew up around Dundas and Elizabeth streets, but the construction of highrises, parking garages, and the New City Hall forced it west along Dundas and north up Spadina Avenue. Toronto's Chinatown has all the dragon kites, paper lanterns, herbal medicine shops, and odors of exotic spices you'd expect of such a district. Stop at **China Court,** an assortment of Chinese boutiques complete with pagoda roof, garden, and bridge.

Turn on to Kensington Avenue for a look at **Kensington Market,** a wonderfully disorganized but amiable street market where jostling crowds wander about looking for bargains in everything from toys to tomatoes.

QUEEN'S PARK AREA

Up wide and pleasant University Avenue, which is embellished by greenery and statuary, you'll come to oval **Queen's Park,** whose cen-

Yorkville is perfect for a stroll—or a long chat.

trepieces are the pink sandstone **Provincial Parliament Building** and other government edifices. Guided tours of the halls and chambers take in exhibits of the development of parliamentary government and displays of Ontario minerals.

On the south side of the park, the curved, mirrored building that catches your eye is the **Ontario Hydro** building, housing offices of the government water and electricity board. It is in itself an ecological example, as it is lit and heated from underground thermal reservoirs.

West of Queen's Park is the **University of Toronto,** widely considered Canada's top university and one of the best in North America. Its medical school is renowned, especially since the discovery of insulin here in 1921 by Frederick Banting and Charles Best.

The university buildings represent an assortment of architectural styles from Gothic and Victorian to modern. You can't fail to note the enormous and quite handsome multifaceted contemporary **Robarts Library.**

A 20-minute walk west of here, on Markham Street, is **Markham Village,** a block of antiques shops, bookstores, art galleries, and restaurants, housed in Victorian buildings restored by mogul Mirvish. Honest Ed's, between Bathurst and Bloor on Markham, is a curiosity of a discount store opened by Mirvish soon after he arrived from Lithuania. Behind the gaudiness and the punning signs—"Only the floors are crooked!"—there are some good buys here.

YORKVILLE AREA

Lying off Avenue Road, **Yorkville** is a great strolling neighbourhood, crowded with boutiques and cafés. Once a hippie hangout, reformed and renovated Yorkville is now almost self-consciously chic, with a well-dressed population promenading around the pretty houses. Cumberland Court and

Hazelton Lanes are the most delightful and exclusive malls within the area.

Not far from here, on Yonge, one block north of Bloor, you'll come to the stunning **Metro Toronto Reference Library,** a massive red-brick-and-glass building designed by Raymond Moriyama, the architect who masterminded the Ontario Science Centre. The interior is breathtaking: a light-filled atrium several stories high, decorated in shades of burnt orange and embellished by luxuriant greenery as well as a fountain and pond. A plexiglass elevator travels silently between floors.

The Annex, a few blocks west of Yorkville, is a more laid-back version of Yorkville, home to intellectuals, artists, and "yuppies." Naturally, The Annex has its share of restaurants and cafés, movie theatres, and art galleries.

North of The Annex, **Casa Loma,** 1 Austin Terrace, is something of a curiosity. Some call it a marvel, others a Neo-Gothic monstrosity; whatever you may think, you certainly won't deny it's impressive.

Fascinated by medieval castles, financier Sir Henry Pellatt built the 98-room mansion between 1905 and

Casa Loma: a medieval fantasy come true, just west of Yorkville.

1911 at a cost of $3.5 million. It took him quite a few years just to collect the materials needed to build Casa Loma. After examining the techniques used in the construction of Old-World castles, he chose his oak and walnut from North America; teak was sent from Asia; and the paneling, as well as marble and glass, came from Europe. Even the huge wall around the 2½-hectare (6-acre) grounds required special treatment—stonemasons were brought across from Scotland to do the job.

With all the terraces, massive walls, and echoing rooms, Casa Loma isn't exactly cozy. But you can admire Pellatt's sense of the grandiose in the paneled Oak Room (which took European artisans three years to complete) and the stained-glass dome, marble floors, and Italianate bronze doors of the Conservatory. Peacock Alley, a hall with carved oak walls, takes its name and shape from one in Windsor Castle. If that's not enough, take the 800-metre (2,500-foot) tunnel from the wine cellar to the stables, where the horses were royally housed in a setting of Spanish tile and mahogany. You can also follow the financier's secret escape route—a hidden staircase leading from his study.

TORONTO'S NEIGHBOURHOODS

The real Toronto is perhaps to be found in its many ethnic neighbourhoods, away from the downtown city centre. Northwest of Casa Loma, at Dufferim and St. Clair Avenue West, is the heart of Toronto's **Little Italy.** Another nearby neighbourhood is **Forest Hill,** bounded by Bathurst and Avenue Road and St. Clair and Eglinton. Forest Hill's population is divided evenly between Jewish and Gentile. There are many beautiful homes in the area.

East of Jarvis Street, toward the Don River, **Cabbagetown** is the memorable name given to an area once described as the "largest Anglo-Saxon slum in North America." It was indeed a cabbage plot for poor British immigrants, and the streets reeked of boiled cabbage. But in the early 1970s the city authorities started to improve what had become a run-down area. Trendies took note and individuals started renovating houses with fervour. The crumbling heaps became quaint Victorian houses—quarters for artists and actors, hairdressers and yuppies. Boutiques, cafés, and pet shops sprang up, and real-estate prices skyrocketed.

East of Parliament Street, the former moth-eaten zoo has been turned into a lively small downtown farm, Riverdale, which is open to visitors.

Avenue Road, a major artery leading north of town, skirts the buildings of **Upper Canada College.** The board of governors persuaded city authorities to leave this venerable private school standing and divert the highway.

There's no special cachet about the Upper Canada College area—it's just a nice residential part of town. East, beyond Mount Pleasant Road and over toward the Don Valley, **Rosedale** is an affluent residential neighbourhood where large houses on sprawling estates are the norm.

Across the Don River on Danforth Avenue (the eastward continuation of Bloor Street), **Little Athens** is as Greek as Athens' own Plaka, with *souvlaki* restaurants and *bouzouki* music. The Greeks have cheerfully replaced waves of British then Italian, post-World War II immigrants, who moved out as they moved up financially.

MUSEUMS

The **Royal Ontario Museum** (affectionately known as the ROM), 100 Queen's Park, was opened in 1912 and is best known for its antiquities from China as well as for its archaeological displays.

In the enchanting **Chinese section,** you will find a selection of beautifully arranged works spanning 4,000 years, from the Bronze Age to the establishment of a republic in 1912. This rare collection was gathered mainly by George Crofts, a fur trader and entrepreneur who lived in Tianjin; following his death in 1925 the collection was continued by the Anglican Bishop of Hunan, William Charles White. From snuff bottles of semiprecious stones and models of a Ming tomb and a noble's house to tomb figures, this display is truly impressive.

The Bishop White Gallery is centred on several Buddhist and Taoist frescoes from the Yuan Dynasty, with outstanding polychromatic and gilt wooden Buddhist deities in larger-than-life size.

There are many other good exhibits, ranging from ancient Egyptian art (along with a mummy) to Etruscan gold objects, medieval silver, and European decorative arts.

Upstairs, you won't want to miss the natural history section, especially the dinosaurs. Skeletons of these extinct creatures—mainly unearthed in Alberta—are set in re-creations of their natural habitat.

The unmistakable dome of the **McLaughlin Planetarium** is right next door to the ROM.

Distinctive bronzes on display at the Henry Moore Sculpture Centre.

The planetarium now houses a new **Children's Museum** which opened in 1998.

The **George R. Gardiner Museum of Ceramic Art,** 111 Queen's Park (across from the ROM and opened in March 1984), contains a magnificent collection assembled by financier Gardiner in a mere seven years. The building cost an estimated $6 million, the collection $16 million; experts agree that the exhibits excellent. Viewing the collection is a ceramics course in itself, with the different production methods from 2000 B.C. right up to the 18th century carefully documented.

The pre-Columbian displays are exemplary, particularly objects from shaft-tomb cultures, whose figures and other earthenware items show a high degree of artistry.

The dinosaur exhibit in the natural history section of the Bishop White Gallery is not to be missed.

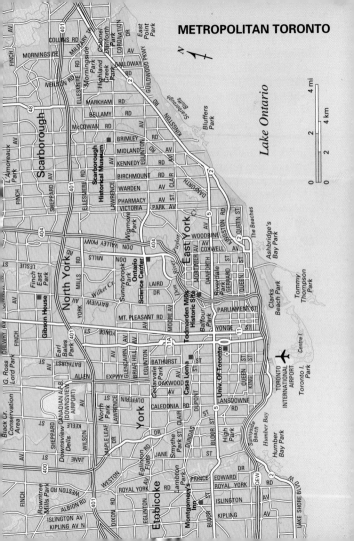

METROPOLITAN TORONTO

Lake Ontario

The dazzling display of European pottery contains Renaissance works from the Medici factory. The Italian style of the era is Majolica—earthenware glazed white with tin oxide and richly decorated with paint taken from metallic pigments. Alongside are 16th- and 17th-century Delftware items—the Dutch equivalent of Majolica.

Europe's answer to Oriental porcelain is also catalogued, with articles made in both hard-paste and soft-paste porcelain. Production mushroomed several years after the Meissen factories were set up in Germany (1710), when the hitherto secret method of making porcelain became generally known. Harlequin and Columbine are colourfully depicted in scenes from the Italian comedic tradition, the Commedia dell'Arte. Meissen and Worcester porcelain here include items made with a yellow background, a comparatively rare feature, given the difficulty of achieving the colour.

Outside the **Art Gallery of Ontario,** 317 Dundas Street West, you are greeted by a pair of brooding Henry Moore bronzes—*Large Two Forms.* Inside, a whole wing is taken up by the Henry Moore Sculpture Centre, opened in 1974. This is the world's largest group of works by the English sculptor, most of it donated by Moore and his wife, who both loved Toronto. More than 600 works are displayed; Moore himself designed the main gallery, using natural light to enhance the monumental casts used for many of his celebrated bronzes.

In a different vein, the European collection is also wonderful. Don't miss the beautiful and truly funny series of proverbs painted by Brueghel the Younger. There are also canvases by Tintoretto, Gainsborough, Rembrandt, Renoir, Gauguin, Picasso, and others. You will see a fine collection of late 19th- and early-20th-century sculpture in the Walker Gallery.

No less important is the Canadian collection, in an extension. This is one of the most comprehensive collections of

Canadian art in existence. Fine examples of the paintings of the Group of Seven (see page 53) hang alongside works by contemporary artists. Particularly representative of the landscape styles of the Group are *The West Wind,* by Tom Thomson, and *Above Lake Superior,* by Lawren Harris.

The Art Gallery of Toronto has recently been renovated and expanded; audiovisual and computer presentations now provide additional information for the visitor. Also, don't miss **The Grange** (1817), an historic house next to the gallery. As Toronto's oldest brick building and the gallery's first permanent space, it gives insight into mid-19th-century Toronto life.

AROUND TORONTO

Ontario Science Centre

Ten km (7 miles) northeast of downtown, at 770 Don Mills Road, lies the Science Centre, nestling in a ravine on the Don River Valley. With over 800 exhibits in ten large exhibit halls, the centre is a dazzling, high-tech palace of marvels. Young and old alike are so eager to play the scientific games that they hardly notice the fabulous building designed by Raymond Moriyama, which takes advantage of, rather than destroys, the natural setting.

All the sciences have their place here, from anatomy to zoology, and you can learn all sorts of things by just standing around and looking. But what attracts most attention is the Space-Age, push-button aspect. People rush for whatever computer games are available; they press dials to look at planets moving in the heavens; or they plug into demonstration equipment to learn something about balance, coordination, and energy.

The Centre shows you the marvels of science in a fascinating and often funny way. You can make your hair stand on end by touching 500,000 volts and see sparks fly 50 centimetres. Try a simulated moon landing; lose your shadow; talk to a computer; see a laser burn through a brick; photograph yourself in the dark with a heat camera; whisper anything but secrets into the parabolic sound reflectors and hear it all broadcast to the world. There is also the Omnimax Theatre with a 24-metre domed screen to enhance special effects.

Important tips: go early, and try to avoid weekends. This scientific gym is a hot drawing card for tourists and Torontonians alike, and the most popular attractions are usually crowded.

☛ Metro Toronto Zoo

(An hour's drive northeast of downtown; travel east on Highway 401 and exit at Meadowvale Road.) This zoo is every bit as special as it's made out to be: 287 hectares (710 acres) of sheer fun for people and a marvellous setting for more than 4,000 birds and animals.

You can get around on foot by following various paths marked by different coloured footprints (take blue for a fairly quick walking tour of major pavilions in all weathers). Or else the Domain Tram, operating year-round, can get you around the zoo, where animals roam freely. In the summer, you can ride the Zoomobile and get on and off at the stops you choose.

You'll want to visit the beautifully landscaped **pavilions** representing major zoological areas of the world: Africa, Indo-Malaysia, the Americas, Eurasia, and Australasia. They all contain fauna and flora of great beauty typical of their regions. In the near future, the zoo is hoping to open a Chinese region.

The zoo is proud to tell you that this is the only place in the world where the natural environment of the animals is virtually recreated. You'll find Florida alligators slithering in the swamps, Canadian beavers grinding their teeth in the ponds, and Malayan orangutans scratching themselves in the jungle.

Littlefootland brings children into close contact with the more approachable animals, and audiovisuals help increase individual participation in the "animal geography" experience.

A new and popular attraction is the **Africa Savannah Project,** which duplicates an authentic African landscape complete with rhinos, hippos, giraffes, cheetahs, and lions.

It can be a long day, so take advantage of the picnic tables at the rest stops. Just wandering through the zoo-park area is made even more enjoyable by the streams and ponds that spring from a waterfall in the Americas section. In winter you can even ski from exhibit to exhibit, quite apart from taking lessons in skiing.

Black Creek's pioneer-style baking: Grandma would most definitely approve.

Smurf Forest is just one of many popular features at Canada's Wonderland.

Black Creek Pioneer Village

(About 25 minutes by car northwest of downtown Toronto at Jane Street and Steeles Avenue, not far from York University.) From an original farm owned by Daniel Strong in the 19th century, the Metro Region Conservation Authority has built up a lively period-piece village. Authentically-costumed guides demonstrate the activities of the time: tilling the land, grinding flour in the mill, weaving or smithery. From log cabin to "Doctor's House," each residence has its charm, and the country posthouse inn where you can enjoy a home-cooked lunch has the anachronistic but welcome touch of air conditioning for hot summer days. Horse-drawn carts or sleighs haul happy kids around, and throughout the year there are parties for harvesting, sheep shearing, and other seasonal pursuits.

Paramount Canada's Wonderland

(Not far from Black Creek Pioneer Village; drive north on Highway 400 and take the Rutherford Road exit.) This 300-

acre, Disney-style park features 140 attractions, 50 rides, and a 20-acre water park. Highlights include the Medieval Faire, with a castle, pond, the Canterbury Theatre, and a pub; International Street, with pavilions from all over the world offering snacks and boutique ware;, the Happyland of Hanna-Barbera peopled with familiar cartoon characters; and Smurf Forest, home to other tiny characters. The entire fantasyland is dominated by Wonder Mountain, with water cascading down from its heights.

Live entertainment runs the gamut from Broadway musical numbers to high-diving off artificial Wonder Mountain. One thrill is a rough raft-ride through White Water Canyon, where nobody minds getting wet on a summer's day. If you do mind, you could always try one of the park's five roller coasters.

McMichael Canadian Collection

(In the village of Kleinburg, just over half an hour's drive northwest of Toronto; take Highway 400, then turn left along Major Mackenzie Drive). The museum is in a striking native stone-and-log structure in a lush 100-acre forest overlooking the Humber Valley. Robert and Signe McMichael bought their land in 1952, built a comfortable cabin-house, and started filling it with paintings of Canada.

By 1964 the owners had accumulated so much art that they decided to allow the public to view their collection; a museum was built (with state help) adjacent to the original house, and in the same style. The McMichaels still take a keen interest in the collection, although they are no longer permanent curators. The highlight of this exhibit is the largest collection of canvases by the Group of Seven (see page 53), attractively presented to emphasize various styles and approaches—a tribute to the painters' celebration of the Canadian landscape.

The McMichaels also have an impressive collection of native art. On the approach to the museum, visitors are greeted by a formidable Inuit soapstone sculpture of a bear. On view inside are beautiful examples of carvings and totem poles, paintings, and silver- and bead-work by Inuit artists.

East of Toronto

At **Cullen Country Barns** (off Highway 401 take Kennedy Road, about 25 minutes from Toronto), a former professional gardener, Len Cullen, has created a magnificent series of naturally weathered barns selling a vast array of antiques, arts and crafts, toys, and gifts. The Barns also offer several attractive restaurants scattered around. Torontonians come out here to stock up on plants, trees, and gardening equipment.

Len Cullen's first-love project was his 27-acre **Cullen Gardens and Miniature Village,** about a 15-minute trip east by car, close to Whitby. Open April to October, and featuring Christmas events as well, the Lilliputian village is enjoyed by all ages. It boasts old storefronts, farms, and swimming pools, a tram system, even a scale-model fried-chicken eatery — as well as an adjoining miniature amusement park and lake. There's also a full-size restaurant on the premises.

Just over 10 km (16 miles) east of Whitby is **Oshawa,** known as Canada's Detroit, where the name McLaughlin is as famous as Ford. From motorized carriages to the McLaughlin Buick, the company pioneered early motor vehicles, until it was sold to General Motors in 1918. The **Canadian Automotive Museum** at 99 Simcoe Street South documents the history of the Canadian automobile industry with wonderful antique cars on display, emphasizing Oshawa's role in the early years of the industry. Start with the

1898 Redpath Runabout, and work through the 50 fascinating vehicles.

The town's big attraction is **Parkwood,** Colonel Sam McLaughlin's mansion (270 Simcoe Street North), where you can view much luxury and rather erratic taste, and may wander at leisure among the trees, statuary, and fountains in the splendid gardens.

NIAGARA FALLS AREA

Before becoming part of the 14 million-odd visitors annually swarming around the falls, you may want to stop off at

The Group of Seven

The Group of Seven revolutionized Canadian landscape painting in the first half of this century, achieving international recognition. The original "seven" consisted of Franklin Carmichael, Lawren Harris, A. Y. Jackson, Frank Johnston, Arthur Lismer, J. E. H. MacDonald, and Frederick Varley. Before World War I, several of them had worked with and been inspired by Tom Thomson, who quit commercial art to paint Canadian landscapes; he died by drowning in 1917, but his followers banded together.

The "Group of Seven" label was a defensive measure against criticism of these artists' somewhat iconoclastic work, which turned away from the then-current slavish imitation of European styles, deriving inspiration from personal interpretations of lakes and hills. Rocks, pines, snow, and water were presented in new ways, sometimes so schematically that they were almost abstract—particularly in the work of Lawren Harris. The group took in further members and influenced others, including Emily Carr. Although the Group disbanded in 1932, the Canadian landscape-painting movement survived well into the 1950s.

Hamilton (pop. 320,000), known as Canada's Pittsburgh for its steel industry. Off Queen Elizabeth Way from Toronto, you can exit to the **Royal Botanical Gardens,** which are spread out over 1,000 hectares (2,700 acres). Highlights are the Rock Garden, the Spring Garden, and the superb Rose Garden.

Dundurn Castle, off York Boulevard leading into town, is a proud Neo-Classical mansion built by Sir Allan Napier MacNab, a lawyer, industrialist, and politician who was joint premier of the united Province of Canada from 1854 to 1856. MacNab went broke before he died, but the house has been restored to much of its former splendour, with period furniture.

Hamilton boasts an area of well-renovated old houses called Hess Village, as well as a farmer's market and the Art Gallery. All are not far from the City Hall in the centre, and well within walking distance of one another.

☛ Niagara Falls

Coming non-stop from Toronto by car you can reach the falls in about one-and-a-half hours or less.

In spite of honeymooners' hype and commercial gaudiness, the place is still far too awesome to be shrugged off as a tourist trap. The 34 million gallons of water a minute roaring over those limestone cliffs, and the rising white mist, make even the most jaded tourists stop and stare.

The falls were formed after the last Ice Age, as Lake Erie cut a channel into the area below—now the Niagara River, once part of old Lake Iroquois. The water continues to erode the escarpment and, unless steps are taken, it is inevitable that the gorge will be cut back completely some day and the falls will flatten out into mere rapids.

The first European on record as seeing the falls was a French priest, Father Louis Hennepin, in December 1678. He estimated the escarpment was 92 metres (302 feet) high. It is in fact only 51 metres (167 feet) high, but the breathtaking sight is likely to fool anybody.

In the last century the falls became a favourite hangout of hustlers selling everything imaginable to the gaping sightseers—everything, that is, except the falls themselves. Honeymooning supposedly started when Napoleon's brother arrived with his bride after travelling by stagecoach from New Orleans. Today, rapt young couples still pose in front of the falls for a memento photo.

Ontario and New York State purchased much of the land in this area and started to oust the hucksters in the early part of this century. The Canadians have made a great success of landscaping their side with vast terraces, gardens, and lawns, but commercialism is still around, albeit with a prettier face.

The **American Falls,** facing you as you stand on the Canadian side, are 300 metres (1,076 feet) wide; the more spectacular

Canadian **Horseshoe Falls,** named for their shape, are nearly 800 metres (2,600 feet) wide. The two are separated by tiny **Goat Island,** which was named for its original inhabitants.

You can view the falls from above, beside, or beneath. From **Rainbow Bridge,** leading over to the U.S. side, you walk along for a couple of kilometres in the **Queen Victoria Park** area, viewing the American Falls opposite and stopping at **Table Rock House,** perched facing the brink of Horseshoe Falls. Lifts descend to scenic tunnels with portals for viewing the mighty waters from underneath. If you choose this lower vista, avail yourself of the proffered raincoat; it's very wet down there. Around Table Rock House are shops and restaurants, as well as many walkways and viewpoints.

The **Maid of the Mist** is a famous boat, named for a legendary Indian girl who was given to the falls as "bride of the river." The exciting 30-minute boat trip up to the booming waters is both deafening and drenching; waterproofs are offered with the ride.

Several **towers** afford a bird's-eye view, including the Minolta 190 metres (575 feet) and Skylon 258 metres (775 feet), both of which boast other attractions, such as an aquarium, a glass museum, a revolving restaurant, nearby amusement rides, snack bars, and more. The Clifton Hill area offers several museums, with exhibits ranging from hilarious to rather touching: waxworks, the Guinness Museum of World Records, and Ripley's Believe It or Not Museum. On River Road, the Niagara

Falls Museum contains some irrelevant Egyptian mummies among Indian artefacts and nature exhibits. Maple Leaf Village attracts visitors for its restaurant shopping complex and Elvis Presley Museum.

Downstream along River Rapids Road is the **Great Gorge Trip,** where you descend by lift to view the turbulent rapids and see the **Daredevil Exhibit,** whose name says it all; it pays tribute to all those crazies who made it alive, or not, over the

The sheer drama of the falls is enough to take one's breath away.

falls in various conveyances, mostly barrels. One section is devoted to the French tightrope walker Blondin, who made regular trips across the falls on a wire between 1859 and 1860.

From Whirl-a-Port, at Victoria Avenue and Niagara Parkway, you can take a helicopter flight for an overview of the falls. On the Niagara River, the foaming Whirlpool can be seen from a cable car, called the Spanish Aero Car, as it swings 549 metres (1,800 feet) up over the gorge.

Scenic **Niagara Parkway** heads northeast, with stops at the Niagara Parks Commission School of Horticulture, a model show of colourful flowers in season, and the Floral Clock, which has 25,000 plants within a diametre of 40 metres (131 feet). Other interesting stopping places include the Georgian-style McFarland House and the Laura Secord House, which belonged to a courageous Royalist who went tearing round to the British troops one night to warn of an approaching American invasion during the War of 1812.

Beyond these attractive parklands and their picnic and bathing spots, you'll pass dozens of orchards and vineyards set back from the road. This is Canada's prime fruit-growing region, thanks to the moderating influence of Lake Ontario.

☛ Niagara-on-the-Lake

Just 15 km (9 miles) north of Niagara Falls, this is one of the most appealing old towns in North America. The first capital of Upper Canada, it was burned down in 1813 but was soon rebuilt in the attractive 19th-century style you see today.

On the way into or out of town, stop off at **Fort George,** the main British outpost of the Niagara frontier in the War of 1812. Levelled by American artillery in 1813 and gradually reconstructed since 1930, it is manned by "soldiers" in British uniform who demonstrate the activities that went on inside the stockade.

Besides historical charm, Niagara-on-the-Lake is famed for the April-to-October **Shaw Festival,** which started in 1962 to celebrate the works of George Bernard Shaw, with performances by outstanding Canadian and British casts. Works by other playwrights are also staged.

There are three theatres in all, but the main **Festival Theatre** at Wellington Street and Queen's Parade Road, on the edge of town, is worth a visit even if you don't have a ticket for a play. A handsome contemporary brick-and-glass structure with a wonderful native wood interior, it also boasts an attractive garden with willow trees and a pond (a perfect setting for intermission drinks).

Shaded Queen Street leads past Simcoe Park, a favourite for picnics, and on to the old Prince of Wales Hotel opposite the distinctive clock tower. A stroll along Queen Street will take you past clapboard and brick buildings with their share of boutiques and ice-cream parlours to tempt you.

Niagara-on-the-Lake is also home to over 30 wineries. **Hillebrand Estates Winery** offers guided tours, wine tasting, and jazz concerts during summer months.

STRATFORD

This delightful town of 28,000, approximately 140 km (105 miles) west of the Niagara Falls area, lives up to its name in every way. Not only does it host the well-known Stratford Festival from May to November, but it also has a quaint and bucolic atmosphere worthy of the Bard's English birthplace —and though the play may be *the* thing, it is certainly not the only thing to enjoy here. Stratford is just over two hours drive west of Toronto, but many visitors like to spend the night here after a late performance.

Shakespeare would probably have approved of the **Festival Theatre's** spiky crown shape, with its commodious, nearly cir-

It's a perpetual midsummer night's dream in the other Stratford.

cular seating area and convertible thrust stage. Curtain times are announced by a trumpet fanfare played by musicians in Renaissance bloomers, and between acts the audience can relax with a drink on the terrace. But this showpiece isn't the only theatre in town. The Avon Theatre offers traditional charm with a proscenium stage, while the Third Stage features mainly Canadian fare and jazz concerts throughout the summer.

Queen's Park, adjacent to the Festival Theatre, provides a peaceful walking and picnic spot for before or after the play. Stratford's people are proud of the ducks and graceful swans on Victoria Lake in the park. Over the footbridge in Confederation Park, at 54 Romeo Street, is **The Gallery Stratford,**

with changing exhibitions, some relating to Shakespeare, others contemporary art. If you follow the lake to the dam, you'll find a gate leading to the **Shakespearean Garden,** where you can admire the flowers—those that Shakespeare mentioned in his sonnets and plays—as well as a bust of Shakespeare and a sundial presented by a former mayor of Stratford-upon-Avon in England.

Ontario's Stratford is sparkling clean, graced with turn-of-the-century stone or brick stores. Colourful places to eat include several jolly English-style pubs. Don't miss the **Church Restaurant and Belfry,** at 70 Brunswick Street, surely one of the world's most original restaurants. This 19th-century Protestant church was falling into ruin

Shakespeare and Co.

In 1830, an innkeeper named William Sargint called his hostelry in the area—known as Huronia—Shakespeare Inn, hanging out a sign with a picture of the bard. The small village here officially became Stratford in 1835, and the local river, of course, was called the Avon. In the early 1900s a Stratford citizen, R. Thomas Orr, pushed the town council into rebuilding a crumbling dam, cleaning out some marshland, and creating a 72-hectare (175-acre) park. The new lake resulting from the dam was christened Lake Victoria.

Fifty years later, a journalist named Tom Patterson conceived the idea of an Ontario Stratford Festival, similar to the English original, and enlisted the help of Sir Tyrone Guthrie. The 1953 opening—which took place in a tent—was a smash hit. Since then, graced by such international stars as Peter Ustinov and Maggie Smith, virtually all performances have been to a full house. A contemporary theatre, designed by John Fairfield and completed in 1957, won the Massey Gold Medal for Architecture.

when the present owner bought and converted it. The superb stained-glass, Gothic-style windows, the oak-and-stone interior, and the big organ pipes make an impressive setting for the French-style buffets, and in the choir loft there's a cozy bar.

LONDON

London is a medium-sized city of more than 325,000 people, about 40 km (25 miles) south of Stratford, with a newly renovated Victorian-style centre. The city's oldest remaining building, **Eldon House** (1834), now a historical museum, is furnished just as it was in the period.

Another representation of life in those days is the **Labatt Pioneer Brewery,** a replica of the original building, which shows you how beer was made more than 150 years ago.

The history of Canada's oldest regular infantry force is presented at the **Royal Canadian Regimental Museum.** Highlights are the regiment's roles in the North West Rebellion, the Boer War, the two world wars, and Korea.

The **London Regional Art Gallery,** on the banks of the Thames River, is a dramatic modern building designed by Raymond Moriyama. Most exhibits are Canadian, from the 18th to 20th centuries.

There are several open-space areas along the Thames, one of them Springbank Park, which contains a nursery-rhyme-theme section called **Storybook Gardens.** There's a zoo, a miniature train, a maze, and an enchanted castle, and you can get there by paddle wheeler, the *Storybook Queen.*

Fanshawe Park and Pioneer Village, complete with log cabins, carriage-makers, and blacksmith, offers a glimpse of life before the railway came on to the scene. Activities include lake fishing, sailing, and golf, with handicraft demonstrations and plenty of wide-open spaces.

You can go farther back in time at the **Ska-Nah-Doht Indian Village,** 25 km (15 miles) west of London on Highway 2. This recreation of an Indian village of 1,000 years ago has longhouses and a palisade, with special displays and audiovisual presentations.

About 80 km (50 miles) southeast of London is a landmark in Canadian history—the site of the country's first oil strike just over a hundred years ago, appropriately enough a town called **Petrolia.**

MENNONITE COUNTRY

This area of pleasant countryside and villages is the home of the Mennonite community, a strict Anabaptist Protestant sect. Head east from Stratford toward Toronto on Highway 7, which takes you into Kitchener and its twin city Waterloo. Perhaps detour to Elmira and St. Jacobs along your way.

Mennonite life isn't all grim. You can see it at its active best by attending the Farmer's Market in **Kitchener,** which starts at dawn Saturday morning and continues until early afternoon. Here you'll find savory cheeses, sausages, golden apple pies, and homemade honey, along with a riot of flowers in season.

Up Highway 85, Elmira and St. Jacobs are small communities surrounded by Mennonite farms, and their typical country stores are well stocked with local crafts.

Elmira was one of the first settlements, providing fertile farmland for the Mennonites in the early 1800s. Its quaint stores include Brox's Olde Town Village complex. Harness races are staged at Elmira Raceway, and each year the town celebrates spring with the Maple Syrup Festival, just as the sap is rising in the maple trees.

Tiny **St. Jacobs**—which was originally called Jacobstettel—has a touch of Old-World charm. You'll find an

interesting account of the Mennonite way of life on display in The Meeting Place Museum.

To the northeast, more commercial than Elmira and St. Jacobs, **Elora** is a fun place to visit. Its arts-and-crafts shops
are in picturesque 19th-century buildings of local stone and
wood on the main street, which culminates in an impressive
mill-restaurant overlooking the Grand River rapids and falls.

GEORGIAN BAY AREA

The Huronia district around Georgian Bay makes a worth-
while day trip from Toronto.

At **Sainte-Marie among the Hurons,** stockades,
woodsmoke, and costumed pioneer "missionaries" will
give you a graphic picture of a remarkable 17th-century
French mission.

Watch the film as you go in. Its story is roughly this: in
1639 a group of French Jesuits came to this wilderness to
bring religion to the Huron Indians. Aided by the Indians,
the Europeans built a peaceful and flourishing community,
but it lasted only ten years. Rival Iroquois—envious of the
lucrative Huron-French fur trade—attacked, killing thousands of neighbouring Hurons. Then, in 1649, 10 km (6
miles) from the settlement, two Jesuit fathers, Brébeuf and
Lalemant, were tortured to death along with many Hurons.
The other Jesuits set fire to their own village as they hasti-
ly abandoned it, unable to cope with the savage attack that
was bound to ensue. The 300-odd Jesuits returned to Quebec, and contact with the Indians was lost for 100 years.

Today you pass through stone bastions and stockade
walls which open out into a carefully reconstructed vil-

*The charm of yesteryear is captured down to the last detail
at the traditional Farmer's Market in Kitchener.*

lage. A guided tour is informally given by ebullient costumed students playing the roles of carpenter, gardener, priest, blacksmith, and Indians.

You'll see the dirt-floor Church of St. Joseph (now the burial site of the martyred missionaries Brébeuf and Lalemant), the blacksmith's forge, the apothecary's counter, a tepee, and a Huron-style sapling bark longhouse. Don't miss the **museum** just outside the mission walls—a succession of rooms constructed around a leafy artificial waterfall and woodland indoor courtyard. The exhibits focus on 17th-century France and Canada, with fascinating French and Indian artefacts.

A mile or so east, on Highway 21 (on the eastern edge of Midland), you'll see the twin spires of the **Martyrs' Shrine,** a 20th-century monument to eight martyred missionaries, including the Jesuit priests from Sainte-Marie. A pathway uphill leads past bronze reproductions of the Stations of the Cross; in-

Old-Time Religion

The Mennonites are an anachronistic sect related to the Pennsylvania Dutch in the United States. The sect originated in Switzerland in the early 16th century, and members persecuted for their pacifist beliefs emigrated to the New World. They refuse to serve in the armed forces and eschew pursuits they consider trivial and unhealthy, such as smoking, drinking, gambling, and dancing. The men have long beards and big black hats, the women and girls wear bonnets and pioneer-style dresses. The only mode of travel is horse and buggy. Gentle but withdrawn people, they don't socialize with curious outsiders. However, the Elmira-and-Woolwich Chamber of Commerce gives organized regional tours with discreet views of the farming Mennonites' way of life.

doors you can view paintings of suffering martyrs or—more pleasantly—vistas of the surrounding countryside.

Across from the shrine, **Wye Marsh Wildlife Centre** provides boardwalks, while naturalist guides point out the flourishing animal and bird life of the marsh. Wildlife wonders are revealed from an observation tower vantage point or, interestingly, an underwater window. There's also an indoor theatre and display hall.

In the town of **Midland,** the Huronia Museum and another faithful copy of a Huron village illustrate the simple lifestyle of the Indians before the coming of the Jesuits. The village has palisades and a firing platform, and the aroma of drying fish. Carry your papoose by wooden cradle

Mennonite travel, just as it always has been: peaceful and pollution-free.

The Jesuit mission: it hasn't always been peaceful in Huron country.

board, grind your own corn with round stones, or visit the medicine man's lodge if you aren't feeling well.

You might allow time for a chartered boat trip that follows the route of Champlain, Brulé, and La Salle, although you won't be able to take in more than a few of Huronia's famed 30,000 islands.

Another stop might be at **Penetanguishene** (north on Highway 27) to see the British Naval and Military Establishments. These have been reconstructed in the way they were originally built by the British after the War of 1812, and garrison life is enthusiastically shown by costumed guides, who perform their military duties with zeal.

KINGSTON and the THOUSAND ISLANDS

Main gateway to the Thousand Islands, **Kingston** merits a visit on its own, for its magnificent setting on Lake Ontario (at the point where the St. Lawrence River branches out northeastward) and for its silvery-grey historic houses. In addition, it has the ambience of a university town, for Queen's University, St. Lawrence College, and the Royal Military College are all based here, swelling the year-round population of 60,000 to nearly 90,000.

First an Indian, then a French-Indian trading post, Kingston became a shipbuilding naval base in the War of 1812. Fort Henry was built in 1832 as the main military stronghold of Upper Canada, and shortly afterwards (from 1841 to 1844) Kingston became the capital of the united Province of Canada.

The many ways to get around include organized short tours, walking, and cycling—the last perhaps the most fun in good weather. You can often rent bicycles in summer on or near the esplanade in front of City Hall.

Down on the waterfront you can't miss the handsome, limestone **City Hall,** with its distinctive dome and weather vane and a big fountain in front—much frequented by young children.

The green esplanade here has several folk-art and craft fairs in summer. Restored, and with a flowered verandah, the old **Prince George Hotel** is currently more student hangout than elegant hostelry, but is still a notable landmark. Behind City Hall, the outdoor weekend **market** on Market Square is a splendid rendezvous for everyone, from families selling

home-grown potatoes or raspberries to aging flower children selling ceramics. The Pumphouse Steam Museum and the Marine Museum are both on Ontario Street near the waterfront.

The most touching historical site is perhaps **Bellevue House,** on Centre Street past Macdonald Park, built like a Tuscan villa as seen by Victorians. Its most famous owner, Sir John A. Macdonald—later prime minister—lived here for only one year, 1848–1849, with his dying wife and baby. Restored and furnished in its original style, the house exudes both gentility and sadness, as the guides explain how the household was run based on Mrs. Macdonald's needs.

Over La Salle Causeway, you might pay a visit to the handsome **Old Fort Henry,** stony and windy on its bluff,

City Hall is the setting for meetings both official and informal.

and usually lively with student "soldiers" acting out military duties of the last century. Guarded by Martello towers along the waterfront, Fort Henry was never attacked. The **Ceremonial Retreat** is an impressive military show, usually on Wednesday and Saturday evenings in July and August.

Long a holiday playground for Americans and Canadians, the **Thousand Islands** are strung out from Kingston along the St. Lawrence for nearly 80 km (50 miles). If you try counting them, you'll probably come up with about 1,700— from the merest rocky outcrop to islands big enough for a yacht club or two and a smattering of houses.

If you're not fishing or sailing, you can just sightsee. Several boat lines from Kingston or nearby Gananoque offer day or half-day trips around the islands; the steamboat *Empress* even makes a luxury three-day cruise. The island scenery is striking, with dark green conifers and sparkling birches set on grassy knolls amid grey and pinkish granite outcrops. Just as interesting are the buildings. Whether simple shacks or rambling mansions, they're all usually dubbed "cottages." Guides point out Millionaires' Row and the places where Irving Berlin, John Foster Dulles, Helena Rubinstein, and others came to get away from it all.

Your boat will probably pass under the **International Bridge,** opened in 1938 by Franklin D. Roosevelt and William Lyon Mackenzie King. It required 2,600 gallons (10,000 litres) of light-green paint to achieve the artistic colour you see now.

Boldt Castle is considered required viewing. You'll find it either a marvel or a spooky Gothic monstrosity, according to your mood and taste. This turreted Rhenish folly might have been quite impressive, but it was never finished. George Boldt, the German self-made magnate who owned the Waldorf-Astoria Hotel in New York, built it at the turn of the 20th century as a gift for his wife. Mrs. Boldt died before the castle was finished, but today troops of delighted visitors wander around the elaborate stone structure and vast, empty rooms to imagine what might have been.

OTTAWA

Natural beauty and man-made amenities combine to make the Canadian capital one of the world's nicest. It's a striking sight with its Neo-Gothic government buildings overlooking the Ottawa River and green spaces backed by beautiful

Get away from it all on the Thousand Islands—there are certainly enough to go around.

Gatineau Park. And the cosmopolitan population of 836,000 are a friendly, relaxed group of people.

At the confluence of the Ottawa, Rideau, and Gatineau rivers, 195 km (121 miles) west of Montreal and 395 km (245 miles) east of Toronto, Ottawa's site was not originally "capital material." Named for the local Ouataouais Indians, the Ottawa River was used by the French for fur shipments to Montreal. In 1800 Philemon Wright established a settlement here as the key to a waterway route for shipping logs to Quebec. The place didn't attract much attention until Colonel John By came, in 1826, to construct a canal as an alternative to the vulnerable St. Lawrence River. The canal was to be a supply line and troop route between Kingston and Montreal in the event of an American attack. Construction men and lumberjacks arrived, and a rough and roistering frontier-style village known as Bytown soon grew up here, with rivalry flaring up between workers from Upper and Lower Canada.

In 1855, Queen Victoria chose Bytown as the capital of the newly formed united Province of Canada. By siting the capital on the borders of Upper and Lower Canada, she hoped that language and other differences could be ironed out. In spite of sniping by the press and others, who considered Ottawa just a brawling backwater, the Parliament Buildings were ready by 1867. The edict was accepted post hoc, and the city became a dignified, if somewhat staid, capital, with proper Victorian buildings to suit the new inhabitants. When most of the Parliament Buildings burned down in a terrible fire in 1916, the buildings were quickly restored.

While Ottawa remained a rather nondescript city for some years, it burst into bloom during the 1960s; with the arrival of immigrants came an upsurge of patriotic enthusi-

asm—especially for the 1967 Canadian Centennial cele-
brations—and also construction of new buildings.

Today, Ottawa is a wonderful and varied city, boasting
top-flight museums and entertainment, good hotels, and a variety of first-rate restaurants—the last offering a tempting range
of national cuisines, much as you find in Toronto. All official
sights and exhibitions are free—incentive for both residents
and visitors to make the most of what Ottawa has to offer.

Although the climate offers some unfortunate extremes
—from wiltingly hot and muggy during part of the summer to occasional Arctic chills in the winter—the in-be-
tween weather can be delightful. Gatineau Park with its
seasonal change of colour schemes, the blooming tulips in
May around the Parliament Buildings, and the acres of
green stretches along the canal and rivers make Ottawa
truly picturesque.

Ottawa's inhabitants are very sports-minded, jogging
and biking all over the place in clement weather, and skating or cross-country skiing in winter—often to work. This
totally bilingual city (French and English) is a cosmopolitan gathering-place, but those who want a *really* French atmosphere and cuisine cross over the Ottawa River to Hull
just inside Quebec.

In summertime, cheery student guides on bicycle-carts
ply central Ottawa to help visitors and around the Parliament Buildings, which are active all year long.

☞ Parliament Area

The **Parliament Buildings**—perched on a bluff called
Parliament Hill that looms over the Ottawa River—are

*A proud symbol of Canada: a Mountie on guard at the
Parliament Buildings.*

impressive examples of Neo-Gothic architecture, though the Centre Block was largely rebuilt just after a fire in 1916. The 89-metre (291-foot) **Peace Tower** is topped by a 22-metre (72-foot) copper spire. Built as a World War I monument, it is notable for its four-faced clock, a 53-bell carillon, and an elevator which takes you to the top for a splendid view in all directions.

All tours take in the chambers of the Senate and the House of Commons, and with special permission visitors may sit in on sessions—ask at the tourist office. The highlight of a tour is the majestic **Parliamentary Library,** the one place in the Centre Block not destroyed by the 1916 fire. Lined with its 650,000 volumes, the magnificent pine-panelled room is a 16-sided dome, interesting for its

Cyclists know the secret: stay outdoors to make the best of the Ontario sun.

The Parliament Buildings offer a great deal of history and a great view from their perch atop Parliament Hill.

carvings and also for the imposing statue of Queen Victoria, who rather resembles a Roman emperor. The statue is chiselled out of a solid 12,000-pound marble block. Note, too, the replica of the dome in sugar.

The East Block—the only building to survive the fire entirely—is also open to visitors. Here you'll see four heritage rooms restored to their original 1870s state, including one used by President Reagan during the 1982 summit in Ottawa.

Guard duty is a colourful affair on Parliament Hill, with the RCMP (Royal Canadian Mounted Police) ready to pose on horseback for photos. But the daily **Changing the Guard** in summer (June 24 to Labor Day) is of special interest; 125 red-jacketed, bearskin-topped soldiers of the Governor-General's Foot Guards parade, for half-an-hour, from 10:00 A.M. In the summer, the evening sound-and-light shows illuminate the buildings in fairytale hues for a splendid spectacle.

Cross the triangular Confederation Square to have a look at the **National Arts Centre.** This handsome concrete complex was built in 1969 (to the tune of more than $36 million) as a performing arts centre, complete with its own restaurant and a summer beer-garden by the Rideau Canal.

Strolling down adjacent **Sparks Street Mall,** you'll view historical buildings in a pretty, traffic-free setting. There are street vendors and performers to entertain you, and you may well be tempted by the Canadiana, art works, and clothing offered in myriad shops.

A few minutes' walk or ride in the opposite direction (east over the Rideau Canal) brings you to the **Byward Market** area in the Lower Town. After Ottawa was designated capital, this area—named after the canal-builder Colonel By—became a respectable Victorian neighbourhood, but fell into dereliction following World War II. Spruced up for the Canadian Centennial of 1967, it is now considered the popular heart and soul of the city, where there is plenty to see and buy.

Around the market streets you can enjoy quaint Victorian architecture as well as sidewalk stalls selling everything from exotic spices to gadgets and snacks. If you're looking for something more substantial than snack food, sit down to a full meal in one of the many restaurants.

Sussex Drive

This pleasant route leads through north Ottawa to a beautiful residential part of town. To get in the mood, have a look at the elegant **Château Laurier Hotel** (one block from Sussex Drive at Confederation Square and Rideau), a turreted, Victorian-era palace.

Proceeding north along Sussex Drive you'll reach the **Basilica of Notre Dame,** a 19th-century Roman-Catholic cathedral remarkable for its interior carvings painted to resemble stone. Turning onto St. Patrick Street, drive out through **Nepean**

Point Park for a view of the Ottawa River and the 700-seat Astrolabe amphitheatre. A fine statue of Samuel de Champlain overlooks the river.

At 320 Sussex Drive, the **Royal Canadian Mint** runs tours to watch coins being stamped and bagged; reserve in advance.

After passing the Lester B. Pearson building, the road crosses over the Rideau River and Green Island, with **Rideau Falls** pouring into the Ottawa River on either side of the island. The windmill you may notice here is part of the Renewable Energy Exhibit, which shows ways of gathering solar and wind energy.

Next is **24 Sussex Drive,** as famous to Canadians as 10 Downing Street is to the British, since this grey stone building,

Relaxation on the Rideau Canal, a sleepier side of Ottawa.

mostly hidden by greenery, is the Prime Minister of Canada's official residence. Just along the road is Government House, or **Rideau Hall,** residence of the governor-general.

You can drive or walk right in past the guards in British-style uniforms to admire the sweeping stretch of lawns and gardens (open most days, depending on what is happening in the way of receptions). If you obtain special permission, you may be able to visit the mansion.

The drive then makes a circular tour of **Rockcliffe Park,** the exclusive residential neighbourhood that also serves as "Embassy Row." The wood, brick, or stone mansions are set in manicured gardens with views, and the road circles the RCMP Barracks, where the "show" division of the Mounties trains and gives occasional performances; from here the road winds back to the heart of town.

More of Interest

If you have time, visit the **Central Experimental Farm,** off Prince of Wales Drive between the Driveway and Base Line Road. Founded in 1886, this 486-hectare (1,200-acre) research farm offers resplendent ornamental gardens and an arboretum, and showcases livestock.

Laurier House, at 335 Laurier Avenue East, a yellow-brick Victorian structure, served as residence for two prime ministers, Sir Wilfrid Laurier and William Lyon Mackenzie King. The house is shown much as it was when Mackenzie King lived here, displaying even his personal toilet articles, plus many mementoes of his mother and dog — he is said to have communed with both of their spirits for advice on affairs of state.

While prime minister Lester B. Pearson did not live here, some souvenirs of his life are also on display, including an intriguing collection of autographed photos from world leaders.

Across the Ottawa River in Quebec, **Gatineau Park,** a 20-minute drive from the centre of town, has much to offer in the 36,000 hectares (88,000 acres) of lakes and woodland, where deer still roam on the remnants of the world's oldest mountain range. Besides hiking and cycling on nature trails or swimming at one of many lakeside beaches, you can also enjoy views from several lookouts and visit **Moorside,** the former country retreat of Mackenzie King. Tea is served in a summer cottage here, and scattered about the grounds are eclectic statuary and ruins brought back by Mackenzie King from his world travels.

To complete or start any Ottawa visit, you may also want to take a summertime **boat tour** on the Rideau Canal or the Ottawa River, another pleasant way to view the city. Inquire at the Tourist Information Centre.

Museums

As well as hosting interesting temporary exhibitions, the excellent **National Gallery of Canada,** in its audacious new glass premises at 380 Sussex Drive, boasts a vast collection of Canadian art and some outstanding European works, including paintings by El Greco, Lucas Cranach, and later artists such as Fernand Léger, Gustav Klimt, and Picasso. Also of interest is the **Rideau Convent Chapel,** a Neo-Gothic, 19th-century French-Canadian structure.

The **Canadian Museum of Nature** is housed in the suitably striking stone Victoria Memorial Building situated at Metcalfe and McLeod streets. This museum offers an easy-going crash course in natural history, tracing its course from plankton right up to more recent plants and animals. You can't miss the Dinosaur Hall with its handsome model specimens looking natural in their leafy habitats on the ground floor. Models of bear, moose, and antelope populate the second floor, which specializes in dioramas of native Canadian wildlife. Upper floors display similar themes.

If you cross the Alexandra Bridge over the Ottawa River into Hull, Quebec, you'll come to the architecturally stunning **Canadian Museum of Civilization** at 100 Laurier Street. Here, you can trace Canada's cultural heritage from prehistoric times to the present.

Longhouses and totem poles in the Grand Hall display aspects of the native culture of Canada's west coast. In the History Hall, exciting life-size reconstructions of historic Canadian scenes allow you to travel through time. Hands-on activities engage young ones in the Children's Museum. In the Cineplus movie theatre, the wide-screen format enables viewers to experience the sensation of being swept up into the action.

The **National Museum of Science and Technology,** 1867 St. Laurent Boulevard, gives serious matters a fun-and-games approach. There are views of the heavens through a huge refracting telescope, do-it yourself demonstrations of balance and optics, and a plastic bubble with live chicks hatching in front of your eyes. In some ways, it's a small-scale version of Toronto's Ontario Science Centre. Unique, however, is the big room filled with old train engines—behemoths from the great era of steam. Another exhibit contains antique cars in mint condition.

The **National Aviation Museum** at Rockcliffe Airport traces the history of aviation featuring early flying machines, examples from both world wars, as well as the *Silver Dart*—the first plane flown in the British Empire, in 1909. In all, about 100 aircraft are on show housed in three World War II hangars. You can see wartime planes in action on annual Aeronautical Day, the second Sunday in June.

The **Canadian War Museum,** 330 Sussex Drive, is filled with memorabilia pertaining to military history, including skulls that Indians took as prizes, a diorama of the Normandy D-Day landings in World War II, and Field Marshal Göring's armoured Mercedes Benz. Weapons range from Indian clubs wielded during French colonial days to guided missiles and other armaments used today by the Canadian armed forces.

Enthusiastic skier or not, you should take a look at how they did it 150 years ago, at the **Canadian Ski Museum** (457a Sussex Drive). Along with the early contraptions used, other exhibits include changing fashions in ski gear, and even ancient cave drawings. The museum shows the development of skiing, particularly in Canada, in photographic form, with most of the participants the right way up.

Further special-interest exhibitions include the **Museum of Canadian Scouting** (1345 Baseline Road), which traces the spread of scouting in Canada and tells the life story of Scout's founder Lord Baden-Powell; and the **Currency Museum,** in the twelve-storey Bank of Canada building at 245 Sparks Street. This shows how people made out before the first coins were struck and goes on to illustrate the story of currency in Canada and around the world. There are also special activities to keep the youngsters amused.

Also of special interest is the **Canadian Canoe Museum** in Petersborough, which opened in 1998. It contains the largest collection of canoes and kayaks in the world and offers informative displays on the history of canoes in the development of Canada.

Outside Ottawa

Upper Canada Village is the ultimate showpiece in a country that loves to recreate and dramatize the pioneer past. Located to the east of Morrisburg, 77 km (48 miles) southeast of Ottawa, it is a beautiful old town, reconstructed when its former location was flooded to create the St. Lawrence Seaway.

In a peaceful green canal-side setting, enlivened by cheeky Canada geese, you'll find authentic pre-1867 buildings, from the timbered sawmill to the brick-built **Chrysler Hall** which is beautifully proportioned in true Greek-revival style. Lots of real work is being done by people in period costume: depending on when you arrive, you'll see plowing and sowing, weaving and bread baking, and many more traditional activities. At **Willard's Hotel** you can enjoy a homespun hot meal or salad lunch served by waitresses in colonial dress. There are stage-coach and boat rides, and you can climb the small **fort tower** for a good overall view, or look in at the old schoolhouse to see how they used to teach the "three Rs."

The pioneering spirit lives on in force at
Upper Canada Village.

WHAT TO DO

SPORTS

Sports-mad, like all Canadians, almost all Ontarians partici-
pate in an active sport of one kind or another—or at least go
to watch someone else doing it. Look out of your hotel window to see hordes of joggers and cyclists in the city streets.
Hotels often provide full fitness facilities, as well as swimming pools. Athletic and sports equipment is for sale or hire
in several shops in Toronto (especially around Bloor Street)
and in Ottawa.

Participant Sports

A bonanza of courts, both public and private, make it possible
to play tennis without hassle. There are also resorts with excellent tennis facilities especially around the Muskoka Lakes area.
Inquire through the Canadian Tennis Association, 3111 Steeles
Avenue West, Toronto, Ontario M3J 3H2, tel. (416) 665-9777.

There are more than 500 **golf** courses around Ontario, 47 of
them in or near Toronto. Glen Abbey, west of Toronto, offers a
championship challenge in a beautiful setting, but many pleasant and less rigorous courses are open to the public. Private
clubs are usually quite accessible, especially during the week
(if you can prove membership of a golf club at home, you can
usually obtain special privileges). Inquire through Ontario
Travel, 1 Concord Gate, 9th Floor, Don Mills, Ontario
M3C3N6, tel. 1-800-ONTARIO.

No need to go on about it; Toronto and Ottawa get hot in
summer. Luckily there's no lack of **swimming** spots, from
hotel and public pools to the beaches of the Toronto Islands, and elsewhere in countless lakes and among the
Thousand Islands.

All that water—the Hudson Bay, hundreds of freshwater lakes, the Great Lakes, and the Thousand Islands—offers exciting and adventurous sailing. You can even learn the sport in excellent schools in Ontario. For yachting and sailing information, contact the Canadian Yachting Association, 1600 James Naismith Drive, Suite 504, Gloucester, Ontario K1B 5N4, tel. (613) 748-5687.

Windsurfing is also popular; sailboards are rentable around Toronto's beach area and at most lakeside resorts.

With a choice of over 400 golf courses, you're sure to find the perfect place to tee off from in Toronto.

In winter, the **cross-country skiing** is superb, with trails around Toronto's ravines and out into the lake, as well as a big network all around Ottawa—not to mention resort-area trails and scenic uncharted tracts all over the province.

Downhill skiing is big in Canada, the best areas being in the Far West and in the Laurentians of Quebec. Ottawa offers a good complex at nearby Ski-O, several ski centers that are pleasant without being outstanding.

Ice skating can actually be a means of getting around, especially in Ottawa, where people zoom up and down Rideau Canal during winter freezes. For those who just want to try a pirouette or two Toronto has many rinks—including one at Nathan Phillips Square outside City Hall and others at College Park (Yonge and College streets) and Kew Gardens.

Fishing in the wilderness means just that—you can cast your line without another angler in sight. But you can also fish within Metro Toronto (where there's a "million-dollar contest" for stocked salmon) and Ottawa. All over Ontario are log-cabin resorts where you can relax and exchange fishing stories. Hiring of a boat and guides is easy everywhere. Besides bass, walleye pike, and trout, the coveted freshwater catch is the muskellunge, or muskie, a daredevil fish of the pike family that often outsmarts the fisherman, and can reach up to 50 pounds (20 kilograms). There are strict licence requirements, bag limits, and seasons.

All over Canada it is possible to go **hunting,** with everything from bow and arrow to rifle, but with strict limitations to regulate the bird and animal population without endangering it.

Bird-hunters flock to Ontario in the fall for partridge, grouse, and woodcock, not to mention the superb **geese,** which migrate in late September. Guides with dogs are available in some places, although many Americans bring their own bird-dogs. Hunting in Canada doesn't require matched Purdeys or fancy clothes, as it might in Europe — only sporting behaviour and good manners.

In the late fall and winter there's big game to be bagged: whitetail deer, caribou, moose, and black bear. In the wilds of the north, the Ojibwa are seasoned guides.

For more information on hunting, shooting, and fishing, inquire at the Wildlife Branch of the Ministry of Natural Resources, Queen's Park, Toronto M7A IW3, tel. (416) 314-2000.

Hiking, canoeing, and rafting provide endless possibilities for exploring Ontario's forests, lakes, and rivers. Particularly breathtaking is whitewater rafting on the Ot-

Baseball is a big deal in Toronto, especially since they have the Blue Jays to cheer for.

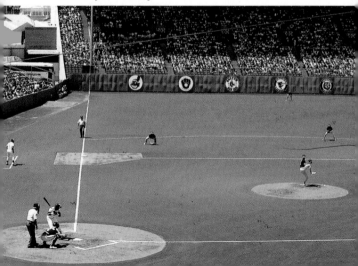

tawa River. For locations, guides, and equipment hire, inquire through the Ministry of Tourism, Ontario Super Host Coordinator, 2275 Lakeshore Boulevard West, Suite 300, Toronto M83 3Y3, tel. (416) 314-0944.

"Dude ranch" is the preferred style of **horseback riding** available all around Toronto and Ottawa, and in the country and forests, though dressage lessons can be found in some places as well.

Spectator Sports

Ice Hockey is *the* national spectator sport, and children learn it as a matter of course. The Toronto Maple Leafs (members of the National Hockey League) play home-based matches regularly from October to April.

Curling usually proves to be a relaxing sport to watch, especially if you have a warming drink beside you.

Baseball gets a big play in Toronto: firm favourites in the city are the Blue Jays of the American League East. In 1992, they became the first non-U.S. team to win the World Series, making them the pride of Toronto. They won again the following year.

Football is played by Canadian rules on a 110-yard field (longer than the 100-yard U.S. version) under the auspices of the Canadian Football League, whose great annual event, the Grey Cup, is hotly disputed in an east-west confrontation. Big-league home teams are The Argonauts (CFL football).

Soccer has become a popular sport in recent years, particularly at the amateur level. Toronto's soccer team is the Toronto Blizzard (North American soccer).

Lacrosse is a truly Canadian sport, although enthusiasm is less ardent than for ice hockey or baseball. Semi-pro games are regularly played in Toronto.

There are important **horseracing** meetings at least four times a year at Toronto's Woodbine Race Track, and several races (flat and harness) at the Greenwood Race Track.

SHOPPING

It's true: Toronto really is a shoppers' paradise. From one end of the city to the other you can stroll in department stores and boutiques, or in underground malls. It's not only an easy pastime (and you don't *have* to lighten your pocketbook), but with the low-key and cheerful approach of both salespeople and customers, it is usually a lot of fun. Most stores accept credit cards, and be sure to ask about a refund (on the provincial tax) if you are taking the goods abroad.

Where to Shop

You won't want to miss the beautiful, glassy pavilion setting of Toronto's Eaton Centre, at Yonge and Dundas, where you can find a huge variety of stores and speciality shops offering everything from a wide selection of fine wines to all kinds of jewellry, men's and women's fashion accessories, homeware, books, and leather goods. There are also plenty of eating places that provide an opportunity to pause between purchases. Another good bet both above and under ground is the famous Hudson's Bay Company at Bloor and Yonge. Specialities are fur and leather goods, but in the mall you'll find just about everything.

At the foot of York Street is the Queen's Quay Terminal, once an old green warehouse that has now been transformed to house two levels of restaurants and boutiques, a theatre, and pricey condominiums. Across the street at 222 Queen's Quay West is the Harbourfront Antique Market crammed on several floors with clothes, antiques, gifts, and much more.

The Downtown Walkway beneath the Financial District is now the world's largest subterranean retail complex, with over 1,000 climate-controlled stores and speciality shops. This kind of shopping is an obvious convenience during the hard winter.

Queen Street West is a trendy boutique area, with shops selling way-out or conventional clothes, health food stores, art galleries, and bookshops galore. The Village by the Grange, on McCaul Street to the north, has boutiques selling clothes and works of art. West on Dundas, Chinatown displays its own wares, plain and fancy. And nearby Kensington Market offers the bottom-line price range in all sorts of goods.

Yonge Street from Dundas up to Bloor, known as the "Strip," used to tout a lot more porn than it does since a recent clean-up. There are several discount houses, and camera and stereo shops often provide good buys.

Bloor Street between Avenue and Yonge is the ultimate in luxury shopping, comparable to New York's Madison Avenue or Paris's

Shopping—and dining— in Yorkville is always interesting, and often trés chic.

rue du Faubourg Saint-Honoré. This is where you head if you can't live without a new Cartier watch, Yves St. Laurent jacket, or Gucci bag.

Yorkville, north of Bloor along Cumberland Street and Yorkville Avenue, has its own chic shopping appeal. The fashions on offer aren't always conventional or classic, but the boutiques are invariably fun, sometimes displaying good clothes by new Canadian or Japanese designers. In these pretty, converted Victorian townhouses you'll find everything: art galleries, antiques and china shops, scent

A little touch of Montmartre found in a Toronto park.

and soap shops, zany gift and greeting-card shops. Don't miss the elegant offshoots here: Cumberland Court and Hazelton Lanes.

Two other areas with many good little shops include The Annex, west of Yorkville, and, in the other direction (around Parliament Street), Cabbagetown. Markham Street is another great shopping area, specializing in antiques, art, and books.

Ottawa has its share of good shopping, with seven areas of particular interest:

Sparks Street Mall—five blocks of open-air pedestrian shopping mall, its colour and bustle heightened in summer by flowers and street musicians.

Byward Market—the traditional farmer's market, with fresh produce brought in as it always has been, and crafts and antiques also on sale.

Bank Street Promenade—a relaxed shopping walkabout in one of the city's oldest thoroughfares.

New Rideau Centre—a three-level mall containing over 230 stores and services, all air-conditioned.

St. Laurent Shopping Centre—more than 240 stores and services with the accent on fashion.

Glebe Merchants Association—nearly 50 stores and restaurants on Bank Street.

Place de Ville—underground shopping for when the weather turns bad.

Canadian Specialities

Contemporary arts and crafts produced by Canadians—often the native people—can be excellent buys for your collection or as mementoes of your trip. Speciality stores and small galleries all over Toronto and Ottawa are filled with good choices for those who keep their eyes open. Exuberantly coloured Indian paintings, wood and soapstone carvings, and the like make wonderful souvenirs. Beaded belts, moccasins, jewellry, and accessories are also good buys.

Less folkloric but still interesting are elaborately hand-knitted sweaters, hand-painted silk scarves, cotton goods such as aprons, new or old quilts, and fancy, hand-finished throw pillows. Another Canadian specialty is semiprecious stones in jewellry or other objects. Amethysts are well worth looking at, as are items in agate, quartz, or onyx.

Furs and leather goods are traditionally Canadian, and come in all qualities and price ranges.

Gift shops galore include all the amusing junk you might want to take back with you—from Niagara Falls, for instance. But even the falls area has high-quality gift and art shops. Most museums offer excellent wares, as do historical sites. A few outstanding souvenir spots are the McMichael Canadian Collection northwest of central Toronto and the Cullen Country Barns at Milliken, northeast of Toronto. Both excel in the choice of attractively presented, locally made wares, including Inuit carvings, brass candlesticks,

See one of the Bard's plays at Stratford, or try some jazz or musical comedy.

scented candles, embroidery, patchwork quilts, ceramics, toys, and much else. There are craft shops in Mennonite country, particularly in Elora, Elmira, and St. Jacobs.

ENTERTAINMENT and NIGHTLIFE

Something is always happening in Toronto and Ottawa, from simple street-busker acts to full theatrical performances.

Concerts go on all year. The late Toronto pianist Glenn Gould gave impetus to all kinds of music, from Bach to bop. Chamber music is a big attraction in all manner of settings, including "aprés-brunch" at Toronto's Harbourfront. Roy Thomson Hall is home base for the Toronto Symphony, as well as the famed (for good reason) Toronto Mendelssohn Choir.

Massey Hall hosts both symphonic and jazz orchestras. The Canadian Opera Company—with its special reputation for excellence in performing Handel works—is usually found at Toronto's Hummingbird Centre in the winter. Pop and jazz flourish in Toronto and Ottawa. Toronto is also Canada's **dance** capital, attracting top international stars who perform with the excellent National Ballet of Canada, also based at the Hummingbird Centre.

First-rate performances of symphony, opera, and theatre, are held in Ottawa at the National Arts Centre.

The Ontario ethnic mix means you might hear anything from Latin-lover music to rock from the German tuba band to plaintive Hungarian violins. In the summer, small towns and resorts are often the scene of Indian dancing, folk dancing, or do-it-yourself to whatever music is available.

Ontarians love the theatre. Most productions are in English, and these run the gamut from state or province-subsidized theatres—where first-run ticket prices are quite reasonable—to avant-garde productions in experimental playhouses. Stratford (see page 59) is as famous on the North American continent as

Festivals

Ontarians find any excuse for a celebration. The following list of highlights covers just some of the dozens of special events held throughout the year. However, as dates and venues change, you are advised to check the times and places with the local tourist office on the spot, or to look in local newspapers or listings magazines.

Muskoka Winter Carnival in early February features crazy winter-sports competitions, such as "snow golf," in Bracebridge and Huntsville.

Winterlude is Ottawa's big-freeze festival, also in February. Centred on the Rideau Canal, there is skating and ice hockey, with snow sculpture and cross-country marathon skiing.

Ottawa's **Canadian Tulip Festival** in late May is a colourful event with four million tulips, fireworks, a flea market, and a marathon.

Niagara Falls celebrates spring with a **Blossom Festival,** featuring sporting events and vintage car rallies in late May.

A **Mennonite Charity Sale** takes place in late May at New Hamburg, with brunch, dinner, and handicrafts on sale.

Metro International Caravan is a nine-day ethnic festival with locations all over Toronto at the end of June.

The **Shaw Festival** in Niagara-on-the-Lake runs through November, staging plays by George Bernard Shaw and others.

On Lake Superior in early July, Thunder Bay's **Round-Up** celebrates the French fur traders' arrival at Fort William with a canoe festival and racing.

Cultures Canada runs from July 2 to September 6 in Ottawa and features performers from across Canada at five venues.

Toronto's **Caribana** is a weekend full of West Indian dance, music, and parades, taking place in late July or early August.

Early in August, Mosport's **Can-Am Race** is an endurance test for racing cars.

The **Toronto International Film Festival** showcases hundreds of films in early September, and is famous for its turnout of directors and stars.

its English counterpart, not only for the classics of Shakespeare but for other genres including jazz and musical comedy. At Niagara-on-the-Lake (see page 58), the plays of George Bernard Shaw are the centrepiece of the summer festival; works by other playwrights are performed as well.

You'll find a huge choice of movies, including all sorts of festivals on various themes, such as mystery, women's films, and so on. To avoid lineups, many theatres allow you to reserve seats in advance.

Informal after-dark activities vary from top-flight cabaret entertainment in Toronto to low-key but enthusiastic piano bars in small-town hotels and resorts. Full-scale floor shows spring to life after dinner in some Toronto hotel restaurants and nightclubs; others sparkle with live combos or strolling musicians.

In both Toronto and Ottawa, discos are lively and informal, and you don't need to know the owner or the password to enter, but you do need money or a credit card.

All over Ontario, midnight is usually the end of revels. Even in Stratford, they're thinking of jogging or tennis the next morning.

The Caribana festival features a parade and other West Indian-related events.

EATING OUT

The ethnic communities have livened up the food scene in Toronto considerably, turning it from a largely meat-and-potatoes affair into a colourful, cosmopolitan pot-pourri. A veritable worldwide gastronomic tour awaits you in Toronto, where there's scarcely a national cuisine that you can't savour. Canadian specialities are still around, however, and among these you can sample wild rice, maple syrup, corn bread, excellent fish, smoked sausage and bacon, or rich apple pies.

When to Eat

Breakfast. This is usually served from 7:00 to 11:00 A.M. Customarily starting with juice or fruit, it may be limited to a Continental-style menu of toast, croissants, doughnuts *(beignets)* or muffins with butter and jam, coffee, tea, or hot chocolate. Or it may expand to a big meal of cereal, waffles, or pancakes with maple syrup, eggs, sausages, or the great Canadian back bacon—a particularly savoury type of smoked pork. Fish and steak may be available as well; the lumberjack traditions live on.

   Brunch. In many restaurants and snack bars, breakfast merges into the special weekend institution: brunch. This may run well into the afternoon, and be accompanied by something stronger than tea or coffee, such as Bloody Marys or white wine. Among the excellent brunch dishes are bran-raisin or molasses muffins, various forms of quiche, eggs benedict (Canadian bacon, poached egg, and *sauce hollandaise* served on an "English muffin"), smoked trout, a fabulous choice of vegetable and fruit salads, flavoured or plain yoghurts, sandwiches, cold chicken, meat pâtés, hot casserole dishes, and much more, including tarts and other desserts.

Lunch. The midday meal may be anything from a sandwich, hot dog, or hamburger eaten on the run to an elaborate Continental-style meal. Serving usually begins around noon and lasts until 2:30 P.M.

Dinner. This is the festive meal, and serving lasts from about 6:30 or 7:00 P.M. until 10:30 or so. Preceding dinner, cocktail time—or happy hour as it is known—is as sacred here as in the States.

Where to Eat

The kaleidoscope of choice—running alphabetically from Argentine beef to Zen macrobiotic—excites even jaded palates. Eating places range from simple and amusing sidewalk cafés up to the grandest establishment, hopefully with food to match the setting and price. Service everywhere is polite and helpful.

Fast food is here to stay, with familiar chains offering up the usual calibrated fare. More fun are the Jewish **delicatessens** and take-out shops, where you can buy a picnic of ready-made sandwiches or fresh salads "to go" in little plastic boxes.

Delis also offer favourites such as blintzes (thick pancakes usually with cream), smoked salmon (lox), bagels

Eat in or take out, fast food often fits the bill in Toronto.

(special bread), cream cheese, chicken soup, and pastrami— savoury smoked beef.

Creperies and waffle houses serve just what the names suggest, with different types of stuffing and dressing—try drenching your waffles in that Canadian maple syrup.

There's been a revival of the old English pub, serving favourites such as steak and kidney pudding, shepherd's pie, and ploughman's lunches of cheese, bread, salad, and pickle relish. Wine bars offer salads and hot food along with a large choice of imported or local wine.

French restaurants abound but of course vary in quality. You'll find old favourites like *foie gras* (goose liver), *tournedos sauce béarnaise* (steak with béarnaise sauce), and *gigot d'agneau aux champignons* (leg of lamb with mushrooms). Also look out for some interesting *nouvelle cuisine* alternatives: *saumon frais à la ciboulette* (raw salmon with chives), *lapin sautée à la crème d'estragon* (rabbit with tarragon-cream sauce) or *ris de veau à l'orange et poivre vert* (sweetbreads with a sauce of oranges and green pepper).

Italian restaurants are popular and usually good. Besides the usual *antipasti* (starters), various pasta, and *prosciutto con melone* (raw ham with melon), you might try *carpaccio* (slivered raw beef with spicy sauce), *scaloppine aurora* (veal scaloppine sauteed with mushrooms and tomatoes), or *involtini di polio* (chicken stuffed with cheese and ham in cream with mushroom sauce).

Asian cuisines are well represented, especially **Chinese** and all its regional variations. From Peking comes the favourite Peking duck and barbecues. Szechuan cooking is usually hot and spicy, Cantonese food is milder, with specialities such as chicken with almonds or sweet-sour shrimp.

Japanese restaurants feature the usual restrained and elegant decor and food, including *sushi, sashimi* (raw fish platters, the former rolled with rice), and lightly fried shrimp-vegetable *tempura*.

Thai and Korean cooking offer delicate and hot surprises, while **Indian** food includes all sorts of curries, as well as *tandoori* specialities cooked in an earthenware oven.

There are also German, Hungarian, Greek, Turkish, Mexican, and Moroccan restaurants in Toronto and Ottawa.

What to Eat

Sandwiches

These are much as you'd find in the U.S.: tuna (tunny), ham, cheese, egg or chicken salad, roast beef (on all sorts of bread), or club-style—chicken, tomato, bacon and lettuce on toasted layers of bread—plus much more, including "deli" styles and Greek pita bread sandwiches with all kinds of fillings.

Soups

These can be anything from consomme to turtle, fish, vegetable *vichyssoise*—the chilled American version of French leek-potato soup—or *gazpacho,* spicy cold tomato-based soup.

Salads

These are often served at the beginning of a meal, or they may be the main course. As well as simple lettuce and tomato, there are chicken, egg, or spinach and mushroom with garlic-flavoured Italian dressing. Chef's salad usually consists of cheese, ham, tomato, and chicken. *Salade niçoise* includes tomatoes, olives, anchovies, tuna, and perhaps green peppers and hard-boiled eggs. Waldorf salad means you'll find slices of apple, celery, and nuts in the mixture.

Seafood salads are usually fresh. Dressings can be oil-and-vinegar Italian (garlic-flavoured), thousand island (mayonnaise, ketchup, and chopped hard-boiled egg), or blue cheese (Roquefort).

The "French" dressing may be sweet; watch for this in other dressings, since the U.S. taste for sweetness has now reached Canada.

Appetizers

You'll find all sorts of exciting cosmopolitan first courses: fish, liver, meat, or vegetable pâtés, quiches of all flavours —including spinach, cheese, egg, and ham, crab, or salmon. *Escargots* (snails) are usually served in their shells, but may also appear in pastry shells; the Russians serve stuffed pastries called *pirozhki* and *blini* with smoked salmon and sour cream, the Italians offer *antipasti* such as marinated vegetables and thin-sliced Parma ham *(prosciutto)*. Stuffed avocados or tomatoes appear on many menus, along with much, much more.

Seafood

It exists here in abundance and is usually fresh. Top shellfish items are clams and oysters, either served raw or cooked with a sauce. "Rockefeller" clams are cooked *au gratin* with spinach purée and *sauce hollandaise*. Find an oyster bar if you want to knock back the fresh bivalves off the half-shell and wash them down with beer. There are also wonderful ways to eat scallops, shrimp, crab meat, and lobster from the east coast—pricey here as elsewhere. Nova Scotia salmon is a treat, smoked or grilled with melted butter. Many gourmets dote on Arctic char, a delicious white fish. Cod, flounder, and halibut can be excellent.

Among freshwater fish, you can hardly go wrong with trout, almost always fresh and sauteed with or without sliced almonds *(amandine)*. Up in the lake country you're likely to see fresh perch, pike, bass, or maybe even muskie (a pike-type fish) on menus.

Meat and Vegetables

Hearty eating is favoured in Canada, and steaks—usually from Alberta—are very good. There are all cuts of beef including English-style roast beef with Yorkshire pudding, barbecued and broiled steak fillets, T-bones, *entrecôtes,* and even *steak tartare* (chopped raw beef with capers, onion, mustard, and raw egg) or Italian-style *carpaccio* with various dressings.

Veal may be served grilled with lemon or cream of mushroom sauce, or cooked with cheese and ham (known as *cordon bleu).* Lamb can be excellent in all its forms—rack or saddle, chops or stew. Roast leg of lamb is often accompanied by the traditional mint jelly or sauce. Chicken and turkey, pork, veal, and calf's liver turn up in various forms.

Canadians like game and treat it with respect. Duck is available most of the time on many menus and may be served grilled, *à l'orange,* with cherries or even with rhubarb sauce. In the fall, pheasant, quail, and venison appear on tables with all sorts of garnishings and sauces. Accompaniments may be delectable corn fritters or wild rice—a Canadian delight coveted even by Paris gourmets these days. Not really rice, it's a grain harvested from marsh

Twilight on the terrace, with a relaxing drink to round out a full day.

grass in swampy areas, a difficult job that makes it a relatively expensive treat.

Vegetables come in many guises in Ontario. Apart from French fries, the U.S. influence has also introduced baked potatoes with sour cream and chives, and France has contributed myriad ways of serving potatoes, including *lyonnaise* (baked with milk or cream). You'll discover all sorts of ways to eat tomatoes, corn (maize), green beans, white haricot beans, snow peas, broccoli, artichokes, baby marrow or zucchini, spinach, peas, cauliflower, and celery.

Cheese

French restaurants offer the best assortment, but nearly all restaurants have various creamy white cheeses, including Camembert or Brie, or with garlic or herbs, plus Cheddar, Liederkrantz, Munster, Gruyère, and Edam.

Desserts

They're varied and appealing enough to corrupt the most fanatical of weight-watchers. But the area around Lake Ontario is a great fruit-producing region, and low-calorie delights in season include luscious strawberries, raspberries, melons, pears, peaches, apricots, blueberries, plums, and apples. From abroad there are bananas, kiwis, kumquats, and passion fruit.

Excellent ices, sorbets, and ice-creams come in dozens of flavours, simple and unadorned or with chocolate, fruit, and nut sauces, or whipped-cream toppings. Health-minded eateries offer delicious frozen whipped yoghurt, plain or with natural flavours.

Pastries range from the most extravagant French goodies (such as eclairs and Napoleons, or more *nouvelle cuisine* articles like kiwi tarts) to native North American pies with short-crust pastry—deep-dish apple, pumpkin, pecan, walnut, or mincemeat (especially good around Thanksgiving and Christmas). Lemon chiffon pie is light and the cheesecake can be excellent: it's made with eggs and cream or cottage cheese plus lemon flavouring, and is often served with a fruit glaze or sauce. Fruit or chocolate mousses make light desserts, as does *zabaglione,* the popular Italian confection of egg whipped and warmed with sugar and Marsala or white wine. Chocolate freaks can usually find versions of the layered Black Forest cake, often with a rich vanilla custard on the side.

Drinks

All alcoholic beverages are available, including popular and fancy cocktails in most bars and cocktail lounges. Canadian whisky (rye) is excellent—although it may take a little getting used to—and less expensive than imported whiskies. All alcoholic drinks, including wine, are very expensive—even in the shops—since there is a heavy provincial tax on them.

Wine lists vary. You'll find that some places offer simple "house" wines by the glass or carafe, while other restaurants stock some great French vintages. Ontario produces wine in fruit-growing country near Niagara-on-the-Lake, although so far they can't quite compete with better French, Italian, or even California wines. The drier Canadian whites are quite acceptable, however.

Canada is a beer-making country, and besides imported brands, you'll find the local and excellent labels such as Labatt's, Molson, and O'Keefe. Good Canadian apple juice and cider are available as well. Besides the usual soft drinks, restaurants also stock Canadian and imported mineral water.

Tea is popular, and tea-time is still sometimes observed as a ritual. Coffee quality varies. You might have to brew your own in many hotels and other dining places. Many places pride themselves on very good coffee.

INDEX

HANDY TRAVEL TIPS

An A–Z Summary of Practical Information

A

ACCOMMODATION (See also CAMPING)

The Ontario Ministry of Tourism publishes an extensive booklet listings several thousand places for tourists to stay, from top luxury hotels and resorts down to rooming houses, in all categories of size and price, located all over the province. Five stars is the top category, providing deluxe accommodations, a complete gamut of shops, services, recreational facilities, and so on. Four stars means excellent accommodations, high standards, and extensive guest services. Three stars is still a high-quality hotel. Two stars means good accommodations and limited services. One star places offer adequate, clean lodging, with few guest services.

Size and type of lodging vary—from large hotels and motels to housekeeping resorts and fishing/hunting camps and lodges. In many towns, including Toronto and Stratford, bed-and-breakfast accommodations are offered by families.

For a free copy of the official government guide, *Ontario Travel Planner*, contact Ontario Travel: Queen's Park, Toronto, Ontario M7A 2R9, tel. (800) ONTARIO.

For information on metropolitan bed-and-breakfast accommodations, contact *Toronto Bed & Breakfast*, 21 Kingswood Road, M4E 3N4, tel. (416) 690-1407, or *Metropolitan Bed & Breakfast*, 615 Mount Pleasant Road, Suite 269, Toronto M4S 3C5, tel. (416) 964-2566.

Another possibility is family-style farm vacations, listed in *Bed and Breakfast Associations and Farm Vacations;* many offer sports possibilities on or near the farm.

Try to reserve in advance, especially for summer vacations. Bookings can be very heavy in the peak season.

Youth hostels: Eleven permanent hostels around the province offer reasonably priced accommodations. For details, contact Toronto International Hostel, 223 Church Street, Toronto, Ontario M5B 1Y7, tel. (416) 363-4921. **Or:** Hostelling International Canada, National Office, 400-205 Catherine Street, Ottawa, Ontario K2P 1C3, tel. (613) 237-7884.

AIRPORTS

Toronto is served by Lester B. Pearson International (formerly Toronto International) Airport, 32 km (20 miles) northwest of the city. Both national and international flights connect travellers with destinations all over America and on other continents. Toronto Island Airport, just opposite Harbourfront, is for small aircraft only.

Pacific Western operates express buses between the airport and Islington, Yorkdale, and York Mills subway stations every 40 minutes, from about 7:00 A.M. to midnight. Regular shuttle services also operate between several downtown hotels and motels and the airport: buses run every 20 minutes, the ride takes about 35 minutes.

Hamilton International Airport, located 68 km (42 miles) south of Toronto on the southwest tip of Lake Ontario, is convenient for visits to Toronto and southern Ontario. Niagara Falls is only 75 km (47 miles) southeast of the airport.

Ottawa is served by Ottawa International Airport, 18 km (12 miles) south of town. A bus leaves about every 20 minutes for the major hotels. Full facilities are available at the airport. Rockcliffe Airport, a few miles northeast of town, serves smaller domestic airlines and is used by private aircraft.

On flights from Canada to the U.S. (international airports), passengers go through U.S. customs as they check in for their flight (and not after they have landed in the U.S.).

B

BUDGETING for YOUR TRIP

To give you an idea of what to expect, here's a sampling of average prices in Canadian dollars. They are approximate, as inflation is ever-present. Prices in Ottawa are generally lower than in Toronto. Note that prices in Canada do not, as a rule, include sales tax or GST (federal sales tax).

Airport transfer. Pacific Western bus service to subway lines: $6. Bus to main downtown hotels $10.75. Taxi to central Toronto about $30, plus tip.

Toronto

Car rental. Daily rates begin at $14 a day and $79 per week. Many weekend/weekly/monthly rental rates are available.

Cigarettes. Canadian $6 for 20, U.S. and French $7 for 20.

Entertainment. Nightclub/discotheque $15 and up plus drinks; cinema $8 and up; theatre, concerts, ballet $15-125 (sometimes entry is free).

Entrance fees. Museums, adults $6; zoo, amusement parks, etc., $8. Children under 12, 30 to 50% less than regular prices. Senior citizens have reduced prices or free entry to many attractions, as do students with ID.

Group tours. Half to full-day tours of Toronto or Niagara Falls $65. $25 for half-day tour of Toronto.

Hairdressers. *Man's* haircut $15. *Woman's* cut from $35, shampoo and blow-dry $30, permanent wave or colour rinse $60. Manicure $15.

Hotels. $70 for lower-priced single room in one-star establishment to $300 double in five-star luxury hotel. Moderate double room $110.

Meals and drinks. Breakfast $7, snack bar or cafe lunch $10, restaurant meal $20, bottle of wine from $15, wine by the glass from $3.50, beer $3, cocktails from $5, soft drinks $1.50.

Public transportation. Subway, bus, and streetcar one-way fare $2. Series of tickets and monthly pass available at lower rates.

Taxis. Drop rate $ 2.50, plus $1 per km on average.

C

CAMPING

The Ontario Ministry of Culture, Tourism and Recreation puts out an excellent guide, *Camping,* which lists over 1,000 campsites by town, with complete information on location, nearest highway access, and facilities.

Other booklets in the series cover cycling, hiking horseback riding, canoeing, kayaking, and a whole lot more. In order to obtain free copies of these guides, contact Ontario Travel (see ACCOMMODATION for the address and telephone number).

Toronto's best campsite is the Glen Rouge Park at the city's eastern edge. It has nature trails and horseback riding and is close to the huge Metro Zoo. There is also a campsite north of the city at Clairville Conservation Area near Downsview Airport.

CAR RENTAL (See also DRIVING)

Cars may be rented at the international airports and in many cities and towns. Well-known international agencies and smaller firms offering "budget" prices have many types of car and RV (recreational vehicle) available. Agencies are listed in the *Yellow Pages* under "Automobile Renting."

For most companies, drivers must be 21 years or over, and hold a valid national licence. The insurance rate is usually somewhat higher for drivers under 25. Major credit cards are accepted as payment.

CIGARETTES, CIGARS, and TOBACCO

A few shops specialize in fine tobaccos, pipes, and other paraphernalia. But cigarettes are usually sold in general shops, drugstores, and hotel shops. Imported cigarettes tend to be slightly more expensive than locally-made brands.

CLIMATE and CLOTHING

Though summer days tend to be hot and dry to muggy (especially around Toronto), you may hit a cool period—even in July—and in any case you should always have a jacket or sweater for the evening. A light raincoat and hat and/or umbrella are necessary, as well. In winter, be prepared for the cold with heavy woollen or fur coats, warm sweaters, hats, gloves, boots, or galoshes. People prefer to dress casually (jeans and shorts are the norm in summer), but for business meetings and better restaurants you'll want more elegant attire.

COMMUNICATIONS

Post office hours are generally 8:00 A.M. to 5:45 P.M., Monday through Saturday, although postal franchises in drugstores and small businesses often have longer working hours. There are two post office locations with Saturday hours: Atrium on Bay, 595 Bay Street, 10:00 A.M. to 6:00 P.M., and First Canadian Place, 100 King Street W., 10:00 A.M. to 5:00 P.M.

Stamps are sold at post offices, and at hotel desks, drugstores, and other small shops with a Canada Post emblem on the window. Mailboxes are red and conveniently located on or near many street corners.

General delivery (poste restante). If you're expecting mail, and don't yet know your address, you can have it sent to general delivery at the main post office. Letters should carry a return address and be marked "Hold for 15 days" (the Canadian postal system will not hold mail longer). To collect mail, present suitable identification at the post office's General Delivery department.

Telegrams. This service is operated by AT&T, Canada, tel. 1-888-353-4726, 7:00 A.M. to midnight.

Telephone. The system is private, similar to that in the United States. Directions for payphones are posted inside booths. Long-distance and international calls can almost always be dialled direct from hotel rooms, but they're station-to-station calls. If you want a person-to-person (personal) or a collect (reverse-charge) call, ask the operator to place it for you. Hotels usually add on an extra charge for calls. You can also charge calls on your U.S. telephone credit card.

The Toronto area code is 416, Ottawa 613. Dial 1 before the area code for long-distance calls (note that some calls within the 416 area are actually long-distance and you must dial 1 or 1-416 before the seven-digit number). Dial 0 (zero) for the operator and 411 for directory assistance (information).

CONSULATES and EMBASSIES

In Toronto

U.S.A.: Consulate-General, 360 University Avenue, Toronto M5G IS4; tel. (416) 595-1700

Great Britain: Consulate-General, Suite 1910, College Park, 777 Bay Street, Toronto M5G 2G2; tel. (416) 593-1290

In Ottawa

Australia: High Commission, Suite 710, 50 O'Connor Street, Ottawa K1P 6L2; tel. (613) 236-0841

Ireland: Embassy, 130 Albert Street, Suite 1105, Ottawa K1P 5G4; tel. (613) 233-6281/2

U.S.A.: Embassy, 100 Wellington Street, Ottawa K1P 5A1; tel. (613) 238-5335

Great Britain: High Commission, 80 Elgin Street, Ottawa K1P 5K7; tel. (613) 237-1530

New Zealand: High Commission, Suite 727, Metlife Centre, 99 Bank Street, Ottawa K1P 6G3; tel. (613) 238-5991

South Africa: Embassy, 130 Albert Street, Suite 700, Ottawa K11P 5G4; tel. (613) 744-0330

CONVERSION CHARTS

(For fluid measures, see DRIVING)

Length

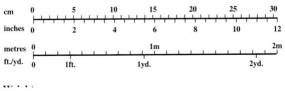

Toronto

Weight

grams	0	100	200	300	400	500	600	700	800	900	1kg
ounces	0	4	8	12	1lb	20	24	28	2lb		

Temperature

°C	-30 -25 -20 -15 -10 -5 0 5 10 15 20 25 30 35 40 45
°F	-20 -10 0 10 20 30 40 50 60 70 80 90 100 110

Canada uses the metric system for most measurements. You'll see road signs marked in kilometres, not miles. Weather reports are given in Celsius and Fahrenheit. Food and clothes may be measured by both the metric and American/British systems.

CRIME and SAFETY

While Toronto is still known for its miraculously low crime rate compared to other big cities, you're still advised to take the usual precautions. Be on the lookout for pickpockets in crowded concourses and the subway, lock your car and hotel room, and deposit valuables in the hotel safe.

CUSTOMS and ENTRY FORMALITIES

U.S. citizens must have some type of identification and proof of address (voter registration card, birth certificate, or passport) to show the Canadian officials when entering and the U.S. authorities when returning. A driver's license is not accepted as identification. British subjects can no longer enter on a British Visitor's Passport. They, as well as citizens of most European and Commonwealth countries (including Australia and New Zealand), need a full passport—but no visa—to enter Canada. It's also necessary to have a return, or onward, ticket and enough money to cover your stay.

The following chart shows what main duty-free items you may take into Canada and, when returning home, into your own country:

Into:	Cigarettes		Cigars		Tobacco	Liquor		Wine
Canada	200	and	50	and	1 kg	1.1*l*	or	1.1*l*
Australia	200	or	250	or	250*g*	1*l*	or	1*l*
Ireland	200	or	50	or	250*g*	1*l*	and	2*l*
N. Zealand	200	or	50	or	250*g*	1.1*l*	and	4.5*l*
S. Africa	400	and	50	and	250*g*	1*l*	and	2*l*
U.K.	200	or	50	or	250*g*	1*l*	and	2*l*
U.S.A.	200	and	100	and	1.4kg	1*l*	or	1*l*

There's no limit to the amount of currency that can be imported or exported without declaration.

D

DRIVING

U.S. visitors taking their cars into Canada will need:
- a valid U.S. driver's licence
- car registration papers
- a Canadian Non-Resident Interprovince Motor Vehicle Liability Insurance Card or evidence of sufficient insurance coverage to conform with local laws (available from your insurance agent).

Cars registered in the United States can be brought into Canada by the owner or his authorized driver for up to a year provided a form is filled out at the border. U.S. auto insurance is usually valid in Canada; if in doubt, consult your agent. Note that if you rent a car in the U.S. to drive to Canada, at the border you'll have to show the rental contract, which must state that the car is intended for use in both Canada and the U.S.A.

European visitors taking their car to Canada will need:
- a valid driver's licence
- car registration papers
- third-party insurance (though comprehensive is highly recommended).

For temporary importation of your car (up to six months), no special customs documents are necessary. But after that, you'll have to pass the Canadian driving test.

Driving conditions. Regulations are similar to those in the U.S.A. Drive on the right, pass on the left. Yield right of way to vehicles coming from your right at unmarked intersections. Roads are generally very good, with enough highway markers and directional signs to make finding your way easy. Toronto is well served with major arteries from every direction, including the famous QEW, or Queen Elizabeth Way, leading straight down to Niagara Falls and Buffalo. Maximum speed on expressways is 100 km/h (60 mph) on regular country roads 80 km/h (50 mph), and in school and central urban districts 40 km/h. (25 mph). The use of seat belts is obligatory, and toddlers must be strapped into infant car seats. You may turn right on red lights if no traffic is coming through from the left, or unless otherwise indicated. When a school bus has stopped with red lights flashing, traffic in both directions must stop.

Things can get very crowded during rush hours in downtown Toronto, around the Gardiner Expressway and Queen's Quay fronting the harbour. Cars must stop at pedestrian crosswalks (marked by overhead signs and large painted Xs).

Parking. It is not usually a great problem, and many parking lots offer space for medium to high prices. But cars do get towed away for illegal parking, so beware. Never park in front of a fire hydrant. In Toronto, there is usually no parking or waiting on main streets during rush hours (7:00 to 9:00 a.m. and 4:00 to 6 :00 p.m.).

Breakdowns. All over Toronto, Ottawa, Niagara Falls, or wherever, you should have no problem in finding help if there's a mechanical difficulty. The expressways are patrolled by the police and often have stopping-points where you can telephone for help if necessary. It is a good idea to belong to a big automobile organization such as the American Automobile Association or one of the two British equivalents—the AA and RAC—which are affiliated to the Canadian Automobile Association (CAA). Membership qualifies you for all sorts of insurance coverage, round-the-clock emergency breakdown assistance, tour planning, and so on. The CAA's head office is at: 2525 Carling Avenue, Ottawa, Ontario K2B 7Z2; tel. (613) 820-1890.

Or you can contact the Toronto office: 60 Commerce Valley Drive East, Thornhill, Ontario L3T 7P9; tel. (905) 771-3111 or (800) 268-3750.

Gasoline (fuel) and oil. There are plenty of filling stations throughout most of lower Ontario, but they are less commonly found up north around Thunder Bay, where you should take precautions and fill up before setting off into woodlands or relatively deserted lake areas. Diesel, propane, and three unleaded grades of gasoline are available. Leaded fuel is no longer sold. Ontario has many self-service gas stations, or if you prefer to have an attendant fill the tank, check the oil, and clean the windshield, choose the stations with service. Many stations also have clean eating and toilet facilities: truck stops on the highways generally offer the best food for the money and also keep the longest hours.

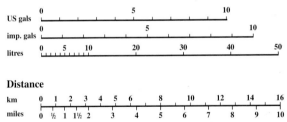

Road signs. In English, or self-evident international symbols. Speed limits are noted in kilometres.

DRUGS

It seems there were once some problems in various parts of Toronto, but if there are now, it certainly isn't obvious. Narcotics squads don't go around making frequent raids, but customs officials are very attentive, and if you're caught bringing in anything stronger than regular tobacco you might end up behind bars. In this health-minded part of the world, anything stronger than a few alcoholic drinks is out.

E

ELECTRIC CURRENT

The current is the same as in the U.S.—110-120-volt, 60-cycle AC. Plugs are the standard two-flat-prong American type, so Europeans should buy a plug adapter before they leave for Canada.

EMERGENCIES

Dial 911 for emergency calls to the police, fire department, or ambulance service, all over Ontario.

Alternatively, dial 0 (zero) for the operator in order to get any kind of assistance.

G

GUIDES and TOURS

Information on day tours and private guides is available in hotels and through Ontario Travel Centres (see TOURIST INFORMATION OFFICES).

Toronto. Apart from numerous guided bus tours, Toronto features walking tours and boat tours around the harbour.

Ottawa. Guides are available around Parliament Hill all year round, and bike around the centre of town all summer to answer your questions and give advice. In summer, free downtown walking tours leave every 15 minutes from the Visitor Centre and Elgin and Sparks streets. For an unusual angle on the city, take a Capital Trolley Tour—an hour-and-a-half guided bilingual tour by trolley bus. There are also riverboat and seaplane tours.

Niagara Falls. Guided tours on foot (raincoats and boots provided) or by limousine, double-decker bus, boat, or helicopter.

Hamilton. City bus tours leave from downtown, where the major shopping area can be found. As the most recently developed entry point for southern Ontario, Hamilton has several sightseeing points of note, including the Canadian Football Hall of Fame, Art Gallery, and 1,000-hectare (2,700-acre) Royal Botanical Gardens.

H

HEALTH and MEDICAL CARE (See also EMERGENCIES)

Large hotels have a nurse and doctor on call at all times. Hospital care is of a very high standard, and emergency rooms generally give swift and efficient service. But medical fees can be costly, so make sure your health insurance will cover you while in Canada. Visitors may also obtain health insurance coverage from the Ontario Blue Cross, a non-profit organization affiliated with the one in the U.S. Details of the plans and application forms may be obtained directly from Ontario Blue Cross, 185 The West Mall, Suite 600, P.O. Box 2000, Etobicoke, Ontario M9C 5P1, tel. (416) 626-1688 or (800) 884-7471.

People with special problems (diabetes, epilepsy, heart condition) can subscribe—for a small fee—to various services which issue laminated cards stating your condition, in case of emergencies, and keep a file of medical history available at all times.

Besides the annoyance of black flies and mosquitoes (and they can be really pesky up in the woodlands and around lakes), there are no special health problems in Ontario. Summer heat and winter cold might be exhausting to anybody used to less extreme climates. If you're going into the summer sun, take the usual sun-screen precautions; the sun can burn you on a lake as fiercely as it might in the Aegean Sea.

Pharmacies, or drugstores, are generally open 9:00 A.M. to 10:00 or 10:30 P.M., Monday through Saturday. If you need something after-hours or on weekends, inquire at your hotel desk.

L

LANGUAGE

English is the language you'll hear most all over Ontario, except for Ottawa, which is almost bilingual, with French-speaking Hull just across the river in Quebec. But of course among the throngs of immigrants in the various Toronto neighbourhoods, you're likely to hear Italian, German, Chinese, Urdu, and so on. Americanisms have definitely crept into this once very Scottish and British part of the world, although in many cases British rather than American terms are still used.

LEGAL HOLIDAYS

When a holiday falls on a Sunday, the next day is often observed as the holiday. There are eight official holidays, when all government offices and most businesses are closed:

New Year's Day	January 1
Good Friday	
Victoria Day	Monday before May 25
Canada Day	July 1
Labour Day	first Monday in September
Thanksgiving Day	second Monday in October
Christmas Day	December 25
Boxing Day	December 26

LIQUOR LAWS

The only way to buy liquor (spirits) and imported wines is in LCBOs (shops run by the Liquor Control Board of Ontario), of which there are several in every city, usually open 10:00 A.M. to 6:00 P.M., Monday through Saturday. Some LCBOs are open later; check the *Yellow Pages* for addresses. Minimum drinking age is 19. Drinking hours in licenced establishments are 11:00 A.M. to 1:00 A.M., Monday through Saturday, noon to 1:00 A.M., Sunday. It is against the law to carry around an open can of beer or an opened bottle of wine or liquor.

LOST and FOUND

The Toronto Transit Commission's Lost Articles is at the Bay Street Subway Station, tel. (416) 393-4100, open 8:00 A.M. to 5:00 P.M., Monday through Friday.

If your children stray in one of those delightful theme and amusement parks, guides and information services can help you find them easily. People in stores and museums are also very helpful.

M

MAPS

Good maps of Ontario and some city maps are available from the Ministry of Tourism (see TOURIST INFORMATION OFFICES).

MEDIA

Worldwide news coverage is excellent, and Toronto itself has three thriving dailies, *The Globe and Mail, The Sun,* and *The Toronto Star.* At most newsstands, many in hotels, you can purchase a wide variety of dailies and weekly magazines from New York, London, Paris, and other parts of the world. In better hotels, room service delivers the paper of your choice along with breakfast.

MONEY

Currency. Both official languages, English and French, appear on the Canadian dollar; all bills are the same size, but the several denominations are of different colours. *Coins:* 1, 5, 10, 25, and 50 cents, 1 dollar ("looney") and two dollar ("twoney"). *Bills:* 5, 10, 20, 50,100, 500 and 1,000 dollars.

The Canadian coin names under one dollar are similar to the American: penny, nickel, dime, quarter, and half-dollar.

Banks and currency-exchange offices. Standard banking hours are 10:00 A.M. to 4:00 P.M. Monday through Thursday; 10:00 A.M. to 6:00 P.M. Friday. Most trust companies are open 9:00 A.M. to 5:00 P.M. weekdays and on Saturday mornings. Many banks have branches with extended evening and Saturday hours as well as bank machines for customer convenience. The best exchange rate, no matter what the currency, is at banks, although some major hotels will exchange U.S. currency and traveller's cheques.

When changing money or traveller's cheques, ask for 5- to 20-dollar bills, which are accepted everywhere, as some establishments do not take larger banknotes. For transactions of this sort, take your passport, for identification.

Credit cards and traveller's cheques. The major credit cards and well-known traveller's checks in Canadian—not U.S.—dollars are accepted throughout Canada at banks, hotels, restaurants, most shops, and many filling stations. Carry some official identification.

Sales tax. A provincial sales tax is added to the purchase price of most goods, including hotel and restaurant bills in some cases. In addition, a 7% federal sales tax applies to all goods and services bought in Canada. Visitors can claim a partial rebate of this tax by acquiring the relevant form at customs on leaving Canada.

P

PETS

Cats and dogs entering from the United States must be accompanied by a certificate signed by a vet declaring that the animal has been vaccinated against rabies within the preceding 36 months. Pets from other countries may be subject to special regulations, so it's best to check with a Canadian consulate or information service before you leave home. On return to Great Britain or Ireland, a dog will have to be kept in quarantine for six months; the United States reserves the right to quarantine returning animals as well. Some large hotels allow animals, and may even have special kennels, but it's best to check on their rules in advance.

PHOTOGRAPHY

All kinds of film, cameras and photographic equipment are readily available in towns and cities, although sometimes slightly more expensive than in the United States. Inquire about camera discount houses, such as those around Yonge Street in Toronto. Camera shops usually give the fastest development service, though you can sometimes find 24-hour processing in drugstores as well.

POLICE (See also EMERGENCIES)

Of all police forces, the federal RCMP (Royal Canadian Mounted Police, or "Mounties") are the most colourful, in their red coats and big hats. You'll see them frequently in Ottawa, but hardly anywhere else, in those scarlet ceremonial uniforms. The RCMP provide the federal policing as well as the provincial and territorial policing, by contract, in all of Canada except the provinces of Quebec and Ontario. Around Ontario, you will see the Ontario Provincial Police, wearing blue uniforms, patrolling in black-and-white cars. Toronto's force is the Metropolitan Toronto Police, wearing blue, usually driving white cars.

R

RADIO and TELEVISION

CBC (Canadian Broadcasting Corporation) is the biggest broadcaster in both media, but it does not have a monopoly. Most hotels have television in the room, and you can enjoy a variety of stations and networks from both the United States and Canada. Both Ottawa and Toronto have radio FM-stereo networks specializing in classical or jazz programs.

RELIGIOUS SERVICES

Almost every type of religion and religious sect is represented in Toronto. Protestants and Roman Catholics hold a clear majority, but there are also mosques, synagogues, and Hindu and Buddhist temples. Your hotel desk and the weekend newspapers can help you find out addresses and times of services.

T

TIME DIFFERENCES

Most of Ontario, including Toronto, Ottawa, and Niagara Falls, is on Eastern Time, the same as New York and the entire U.S. East Coast. Regions west of 90° longitude, around Thunder Bay, are on Central Time, one hour earlier. The first Sunday in April marks the start of Daylight Saving Time, when clocks are advanced one hour. Clocks are turned back one hour at the end of Daylight Saving Time on the last Saturday in October.

Los Angeles	Chicago	**Toronto**	Halifax	London	Paris
9:00 A.M.	11:00 A.M.	**noon**	1:00 P.M.	5:00 P.M.	6:00 P.M.

TIPPING

As in the United States, a service charge is not normally included in hotel and restaurant bills, so tipping is customary. You may use your discretion, but here are some guidelines:

Hotel porter, per bag	75¢
Maid, per day	$1-2
Waiter	15%
Hairdresser/barber	10-15%
Taxi driver	10-15%
Tour guide	10%

TOILETS

Ontarians will probably understand you if you ask for the "rest-room," "washroom," "lavatory," "loo," or "john." Nowadays these conveniences are usually marked with pictographs for men or women. They are mostly clean and easily found in filling stations, museums, subway stops, and cafés or bars (where they'd rather you buy a drink), as well as the shopping complexes, above or below ground. If there are attendants, you should leave a tip.

TOURIST INFORMATION OFFICES

The Ontario Ministry of Tourism and the Canadian Government Office of Tourism operate information services in many countries. They will supply a host of brochures and maps covering everything from hotels and transportation to special vacations and accommodations.

Canadian Government offices abroad:

Australia: Consulate General of Canada, Level 5, Quay West Building, 111 Harrington Street, Sydney NSW 2000, tel. (612) 9-364-3000

Great Britain: MacDonald House, 1 Grosvenor Square, London W1X OAB; tel. (171) 258-6600

U.S.A.: offices are in most major cities.

For information on **Canada:**
   Tourism Canada, 1 Concorde Gate, 9th Floor, Don Mills, Ontario, M3C 3N6, tel. (416) 445-5663, or (800) 577-2266, 8:00 A.M. to 8:00 P.M. Monday through Friday

For information on **Ontario:**
   Hearst Block, 900 Bay Street, Toronto, Ontario M7A 2E1; tel. (416) 314-0944 Monday through Friday 8:00 A.M. to 6:00 P.M. (open extended hours in summer). Toll-free from U.S. (800) ONTARIO (668-2746). They also have an office in the Eaton Centre, 220 Yonge Street, in Eaton's, Level 1, Monday to Friday, 10:00 A.M. to 9:00 P.M., Saturday, 9:30 A.M. to 6:00 P.M., Sunday noon to 5:00 P.M.

Tourist information in Toronto and Ottawa:
Metropolitan Toronto Convention and Visitor's Association, Queen's Quay Terminal at Harbourfront, P.O. Box 126, 207 Queen's Quay West, Suite 590, Toronto, Ontario M5J 1A7; tel. (416) 203-2500; (800) 363-1990, Monday through Friday 8:30 A.M. to 4:30 P.M. (later hours in summer), Saturdays 9:00 A.M. to 5:00 P.M. and Sundays 10:00 A.M. to 5:00 P.M.

   During the summer, there are information booths outside the Art Gallery of Ontario and the Royal Ontario Museum.

   Ottawa Tourism and Convention Authority (OTCA), Visitor Information Centre, 130 Albert Street, Suite 1800, Ottawa, K1P 5G4, tel. (613) 237-6822, 5 days, daytime only.

   National Capital Commission Centre, 202-40 Elgin Street, Ottawa K1P 1C7, tel. (613) 239-5000 or (800) 465-1867, 7 days, 8:00 A.M. to 8:00 P.M.

TRANSPORTATION

Toronto. The Toronto Transit Commission (TTC) assures easy travel around town even if you aren't driving yourself. The efficient, safe, and clean subway (underground) is renowned; it covers the city in a north-south loop, plus lines east and west. Hours: 7:00 A.M. to 10:00 P.M., 7 days a week. Tel. (416) 393-4636.

Buses and streetcars cover the city quite thoroughly. You can get a free transfer if you need both subway and bus or streetcar one way from A to B. Buses accept only exact fare or ticket-transfer bought in subway stations. The Queen, College, and St. Clair streetcars and some buses run 24 hours a day.

Ferry service. Transportation to Niagara has been upgraded with a high-speed ferry service. The state-of-the-art 300-passenger ship docks at Jordan Harbour, where a shuttle service can take visitors directly to Niagara-on-the-Lake, Casino Niagara, or Niagara Falls. Contact Waterways Transportation Services Corporation, (888) 581-2628, fax (416) 203-1413.

Ottawa. Bus routes are operated by the Ottawa-Carleton Regional Transit Commission (OC TRANSPO), offering maps in their main office at 294 Albert Street. If you don't have the required one-way exact fare, you can buy tickets at some tobacco and other shops.

Taxis are readily available at taxi stands, especially near hotels, important concourses, railroad stations, and so on. They can also be hailed in the street or phoned from your hotel or elsewhere.

Trains. GO (Government of Ontario) Transit services connect Toronto's Union Station with the outer suburbs, as far as Hamilton; tel. (416) 665-0022. Buses also, outside town.

VIA Rail operates all over Canada. The Toronto terminal is Union Station at Bay and Front streets; tel. (416) 366-8411. The Ottawa terminal is on St. Laurent Boulevard, a good way southeast of the city centre; tel. (613) 244-8289.

WATER

Tap water is safe to drink. Most hotels and motels provide an ice machine in the corridor or stairwell, often alongside a soft-drink dispenser. Well-known brands of mineral water can be purchased in shops and markets as well as in better restaurants.

Recommended Hotels

It is very difficult to find a good hotel in downtown Toronto; the city is notoriously expensive and the hotels are no exception. Bed-and-breakfast, university dorms, or hostels are the best answer if you have to be frugal. Don't forget to ask about the special packages offered through airlines, groups, or even credit cards. They can save you a bundle. If you are not so frugal, there are some beautiful landmark hotels to choose from.

Listed below is a selection of hotels in four price categories. As a basic guide we have used the symbols below to indicate prices for a double room with bath, including breakfast:

✪	below C$90
✪✪	C$90–120
✪✪✪	C$120–160
✪✪✪✪	over C$160

Be prepared to pay the 5% accommodations tax and the national 7% GST. A refund for both taxes is available to foreign visitors, providing the receipts are saved and the appropriate refund form is filed. Note that the prices above do not include these taxes.

DOWNTOWN

Best Western Primrose Hotel ✪✪ *111 Carlton Street, M5B 2G3; Tel. (416) 977 8000 or (800) 268 8082, fax (416) 977 6323.* Large, comfortable rooms, usually with two double beds. Very nice Viennese-style café. Room service from 7 A.M. to 10 P.M. Complimentary newspaper available; outdoor pool and sauna. Weekend packages available (except during summer months). 338 rooms, 4 suites. Major credit cards.

Bond Place Hotel ✪-✪✪ *65 Dundas Street E., M5B 2G8; Tel. (416) 362 6062, fax (416) 360 6406.* Good downtown location at reasonable prices. The decor is dated but well-kept. Room service from 7 A.M. to 10 P.M.; laundry and valet service available. Weekend packages from December to April. Two restaurants. Valet parking ($C12). 286 rooms and suites. Major credit cards.

Cambridge Suites Hotel ✪✪✪✪ *15 Richmond St. E., M5C 1N2; Tel. (416) 368 1990 or 800-463 1990, fax (416) 601 3751.* Custom-designed to satisfy all the travellers' needs, this exclusive hotel is situated in the downtown financial district as a convenience for both businessmen and tourists. Each suite is equipped with a refrigerator, microwave, two televisions, couch, dressing room, and a fully-stocked minibar. You can also utilize their facilities which include a fitness center with a skyline view of the city, comfortable bar, and more than adequate restaurant. Room service from 11 A.M. to 11 P.M. 230 suites. Valet parking C$16. Major credit cards.

Clarion Essex Park Hotel ✪✪ *300 Jarvis Street, M5B 2C5; Tel. (416) 977 4823 or (800) 567 2233, fax (416) 977 4830.* Located near the Pantages Theatre and City Hall, this is a tour-group favorite. It offers a great deal of extras for such a moderately priced hotel—refrigerators, hairdryers, king- or queen-sized beds, indoor pool, fitness center, squash courts. Bistro and bar. 58 rooms and 44 suites. Major credit cards.

Comfort Hotel ✪✪ *15 Charles Street E., M4Y 1S1; Tel. (416) 924 1222 or (800) 228 5150, fax (416) 927 1369.* Quiet and convenient downtown location. Another good reason to stay here is the well-known jazz piano bar. Parking. 108 rooms. Major credit cards.

Crowne Plaza Toronto Centre ✪✪✪ *225 Front Street W., M5V 2X3; Tel. (416) 597 1400 or (800) 422 7969, fax (416) 597 8128.* Conveniently located near all downtown tourist stops; its very elegantly decorated rooms make this a popular hotel in Toronto. Excellent dining at both the Trellis Bistro and Lounge (located in the garden court) and the Chanterelles. Indoor pool, fitness facilities, and sundeck. 587 rooms and suites. Major credit cards.

Delta Chelsea Inn ✪✪-✪✪✪ *33 Gerrard St. W., M5G 1Z4; Tel. (416) 595 1975 or (800) 243 5732, fax (416) 595 1975.* Great family hotel with babysitting services, 24-hour room service, kitchenettes on request, and both restaurant and cafeteria (children under 6 years eat for free). Adult fitness center and children's creative center for 3- to 12-year-olds. Valet parking (C$18). Children under 18 years free. 1,547 rooms and 47 suites. Major credit cards.

Hilton International ✪✪✪ *145 Richmond St. W., M5H 2L2; Tel. (416) 869 3456 or (800) 445 8667, fax (416) 869 1478.* With 32 stories, this Hilton has large rooms, dining room, 24-hour room service, indoor/outdoor pool, extensive fitness center, and valet parking (C$12 weekends/C$20 weekdays). 601 rooms and suites. Major credit cards.

Hotel Victoria ✪ *56 Yonge Street (at Wellington), M5E 1G5; Tel. (416) 363 1666, fax (416) 363 7327.* For a more intimate environment, stay in this landmark building in the financial district. They offer a choice of standard (slightly smaller rooms) or select (larger rooms) equipped with all the necessary conveniences—private baths, A/C, restaurant, and bar. Room service from 7 A.M. to 2 P.M. Valet parking C$16. Special weekend rates available. 48 rooms. Major credit cards.

King Edward Hotel ✪✪-✪✪✪ *37 King Street, M5C 2E9; Tel. (416) 863 9700, fax (416) 367 5515.* Toronto's oldest hotel, known to locals as "The King Eddy," has had an impressive guest list, including the Prince of Wales and Charles de Gaulle. The beautiful marble columns and the lobby's glass-domed rotunda were restored in the 1980s, making this a terrific place for traditional English tea in the lobby. Lounge. 315 rooms and suites. Marble bathrooms, minibar, formal dining room, small fitness room, spa, and valet parking ($23). Major credit cards.

The Metropolitan Hotel ✪✪✪–✪✪✪✪ *108 Chestnut Street, M5G 1R3; Tel. (416) 977 5000, fax (416) 977 9513.* Recent renovations (C$28 million at completion) have turned this into a 4-star hotel. The dining room, Hemispheres, is not to be missed, because of its star chef Susur Lee. Very business-traveler-oriented, boasting rooms with large desks; also has conveniences like bathrobes, hairdryers, and massage shower-heads. Indoor swimming pool; extensive fitness center; valet parking C$18.25. Children under 18 years free. 469 rooms, 44 suites. Major credit cards.

Neil Wycik College Hotel ✪ *96 Gerrard Street E., M5B 1G7; Tel. (416) 977 2320 or (800) 268 4358, fax (416) 977 2809.* Clean, modern, and inexpensive. Designed for a student clientele, this hotel doesn't offer A/C or private bath, but does have a TV lounge, sauna, and rooftop sundeck. If you want to cook, there are kitchen facilities. Parking (C$12). 304 rooms. MasterCard and Visa only.

Novotel ✪✪ *45 The Esplanade, M5E 1W2; Tel. (416) 367 8900 or (800) 668 6835, fax (416) 360 8285.* Modern hotel built in French Renaissance style with well-equipped rooms (two telephones, minibar, and even radio and TV speakers in the bathroom). While their dining room, Café Nicole, is only adequate, their facilities more than compensate—airport shuttle service, fitness center, indoor pool, valet and concierge service. Valet parking (C$13.50). 262 rooms and 8 suites. Major credit cards.

Radisson Plaza Hotel Admiral ✪✪✪ *249 Queen's Quay W. M5J 2N5; Tel. (416) 878-2000203 3333 or 800-333 3333, fax (416) 203 3100.* Located right on the harbour, the lobby and restaurant reflect a nautical theme. Beautiful rooms with marble table-tops and brass trimmings are complemented by all the extras—two telephones, hairdryer, minibar, and complimentary newspaper delivery. The facilities are also fabulous —swimming pool, squash court, and cabana-style bar. 151 rooms and suites. Valet parking (C$15). Major credit cards.

Royal York ✪✪✪✪ *100 Front Street W., M5J 1E3; Tel. (416) 863 6333 or (800) 441 1414, fax (416) 933-3611.* This is a massive institution in Toronto where many historic and social events have taken place since its construction in 1929. For some, its size is a bit overpowering—over 10,000 people can be seated in the elegant banquet rooms, and 2,800 guests can sleep here at one time. The rooms are appropriately furnished with antique reproductions. Complimentary breakfast; over 10 restaurants and lounges; 24-hour room service. Indoor pool and fitness center. 1,365 rooms and suites. Special packages available. Valet parking (C$23). Major credit cards.

The Sheraton Centre ✪✪✪ *123 Queen Street W., M5H 2H9; Tel. (416) 361 1000 or (800) 325 3535, fax (416) 947 4854.* Large, modern convention hotel connected to a shopping complex, 6 restaurants and bars, and 2 movie theatres. The bonus feature here is the 2-acre garden, with a restaurant overlooking a waterfall. Large rooms, 24-hour room service, indoor/outdoor pool, sun deck, fitness center. Valet parking (C$22). Children under 18 free. 1,382 rooms and suites. Major credit cards.

SkyDome Hotel ✪✪–✪✪✪ *1 Blue Jays Way, M5V 1J4; Tel. (416) 341 7100 or (800) 441 1414, fax (416) 341 5090.* Primarily a corporate hotel. Small fitness center, indoor pool, 5 banquet rooms, and full banquet services. 180 rooms. Major credit cards.

Toronto International Hostel ✪ *4160 Mutual Street at Gerrard, M5B 2M2; Tel. (416) 971 4440, fax (416) 971 4088.* Typical hostel accommodations that include bed, closet, sink, and kitchen. Four rooms to one bathroom and a TV to each floor. Fitness center and pool. Parking (C$7). MasterCard and Visa only.

Westin Harbour Castle ✪✪✪ *1 Harbour Square, M5J 1A6; Tel. (416) 869 1600 or (800) 228 3000, fax (416) 869 0573.* For those who want to stay by the harbourfront, this is the perfect hotel. The rooms, located in two towers that overlook the lake, are handsomely decorated, with marble-top tables. The Lighthouse is a revolving restaurant on the 38th floor of the south tower. 24-hour room service, indoor pool, squash courts, and shopping arcade. Valet parking ($C21); self-parking ($C14). Children under 18 free. Limit 5 people to one room. Weekend packages available. 980 rooms and suites. Major credit cards.

MIDTOWN

The Four Seasons ✪✪✪✪ *21 Avenue Road, M5R 2G1; Tel. (416) 964 0411 or (800) 268 6282, fax (416) 964 2301.* This hotel caters to families, with offers of two hours free at Kids & Quackers (a supervised play area) and free video games; known for its excellent service. Huge rooms and all the extras for complete comfort. Facilities include health club, indoor/outdoor pool, 24-hour room service and valet pickup, babysitting services, and an appealing Mediterranean restaurant. Valet parking (C$20). 210 rooms and 170 suites. Major credit cards.

Hotel Selby ✪✪ *592 Sherbourne Street, M4X 1L4; Tel. (416) 921 3142 or (800) 387 4788, fax (416) 923 3177.* A beautiful

Victorian building houses this inexpensive downtown hotel. Because of the high ceilings in the rooms, they appear enormous and even have walk-in closets. The decor is elegantly antique. Continental breakfast. Access to fitness center for fee. Free parking. 67 rooms. Major credit cards.

Quality Hotel ✪✪ *280 Bloor Street W., M5S 1V8; Tel. (416) 968 0010.* Dependable chain hotel with all the modern conveniences at half the price. Restaurant and coffee shop. Room service from 7 A.M. to noon and from 5 to 11 P.M. Weekend packages available. Parking (C$11.50). 210 rooms. Major credit cards.

Radisson Plaza Hotel ✪✪–✪✪✪ *90 Bloor Street E., M4W 1A7; Tel. (416) 961 8000 or (800) 333 3333, fax (416) 961 4635.* The designers did an excellent job using inner courtyards on the seventh to 12th floors of the plaza. The lobby is on the first level. Children under 18 free. Parking (C$18.50). Restaurant theme is Matisse, complete with wall murals. 238 rooms, 18 suites. Major credit cards.

Victoria University ✪ *140 Charles Street W., M5S 1K9; Tel. (416) 585 4524, fax (416) 585 4530.* Located directly across from the Royal Ontario Museum; rooms are available from mid-May to late August only. Rooms are small but sufficient, with bathrooms down the hall. 700 rooms. MasterCard and Visa only.

UPTOWN

Best Western Roehampton Hotel ✪✪ *808 Mount Pleasant Road, M4P 2L2; Tel. (416) 487 5101 or (800) 387 8899, fax (416) 487 5390.* Recently renovated, these large rooms will suit all your needs for a fairly reasonable price. Room service from 10 A.M. to 11 P.M. Parking (C$7). Facilities include outdoor rooftop pool and sundeck. 110 rooms and suites. Major credit cards.

Recommended Restaurants

There are a wide variety of cuisines represented in Toronto. Explore the diverse neighbourhoods—the East End is filled with Greek restaurants; near Dundas and Spadina you'll find Chinatown; and Little Italy can be found along College Street. And the prices are often reasonable.

The listed restaurants are categorized according to city districts, and use the following price system in Canadian dollars:

✪	under C$10
✪✪	C$10–20
✪✪✪	C$20–30
✪✪✪✪	over C$30

DOWNTOWN WEST

Acqua ✪✪✪ *10 Front Street W., Tel. (416) 368 7171.* This is the most chic restaurant in Toronto, with a Venetian theme. Past its very popular bar is the elaborate dining courtyard. Italian fare prevails, with specialties like grilled veal chops and pan-seared local whitefish. Save room for the amazing desserts—including a spectacular chocolate-raspberry *crème brûlée*. Open Mon-Fri 11:30 A.M.-11:30 P.M., Sat 5-11:30 P.M. Reservations recommended.

Avalon ✪✪✪ *270 Adelaide Street W., Tel. (416) 979 9918.* An elegant setting and elegantly prepared foods. The menu changes daily, but one can always count on the food to be very fresh and organically grown. Choose from some of the very eclectic daily specials—yellowfin tuna prepared with roasted artichokes and Bordelaise sauce or wood-grilled Cornish hen. Open Wed-Fri noon-2:30 P.M.; Mon-Thurs 5:30-10 P.M.; Fri-Sat 5:30-11 P.M.

Babur ✪✪ *273 Queen Street W., Tel. (416) 599 7720.* A moderately priced Indian restaurant that will delight your palate. Vegetarians have a wide selection here. Open daily 11:45 A.M.-2:30 P.M. and 5-10:30 P.M.

Barberian's ✪✪✪ *7 Elm Street, Tel. (416) 597 0335.* For the true steak-lover, this steak house features 10 varieties (including seafood) grilled to perfection. Its early-Canadian decor and selection of more than 500 different wines draw a sophisticated crowd. Reservations required. Open for lunch Mon-Fri noon-2:30 P.M.; and for dinner daily 5 P.M.-midnight.

La Bodega ✪✪ *30 Baldwin Street, Tel. (416) 977 1287.* Make sure you get reservations in advance for both lunch and dinner, due to La Bodega's growing popularity. Locals find this traditional French restaurant attractive because of its comfortable surroundings and fresh, superbly prepared food at reasonable prices. The summer patio is a favourite. Open for lunch Mon-Fri noon-2:30 P.M.; dinners Mon-Sat 5-10:30 P.M.

Canoe ✪✪✪ *66 Wellington Street W., Tel. (416) 364 0054.* Traditional Canadian fare (Digby scallops, Alberta beef, Yukon caribou, Ontario pheasant) prepared in unusual ways. The restaurant sits on 54th floor of the Toronto Dominion Bank Tower, providing an amazing view of the city. Open for lunch Mon-Fri 11:30 A.M.-2:30 P.M.; and for dinner daily 5-10:30 P.M.

Chiaro's ✪✪✪✪ *37 King Street E., Tel. (416) 863 9700.* Located in the King Edward's Hotel, this is formal dining at its finest. Award winning French and Continental cuisine includes roast lamb with lemon-thyme sauce, poached Dover sole tartare with shrimp and capers, and shelled lobster with lemon-honey sauce. Reservations recommended. Open Mon-Sat 5:30-10:30 P.M. Closed Sundays.

Cities ✪✪ *859 Queen Street W., Tel. (416) 504 3762.* This amazing menu ranges from shrimp served with pineapple salsa to glazed rack of lamb—at surprisingly moderate prices. Open Tues-Fri noon-2 P.M., Sunday-Wed 5:30-10 P.M., and Thurs-Sat 5:30-11 P.M.

Filet of Sole ✪✪-✪✪✪ *11 Duncan Street, Tel. (416) 598 3256.* A theatre-patron favorite, with wonderful seafood dishes at reasonable prices (C$14 to $18)—salmon, swordfish, tuna, bluefish. If you want to spend a bit more try the daily specials, such as salmon with horseradish crust. Open for lunch Mon-Fri noon-2:30 P.M. and dinners daily 5-11 P.M.

Free Times Café ✪ *320 College Street, Tel. (416) 967 1078.* Vegetarian's delight with art displays that complement the casual ambience. Folk and other acoustic music featured nightly. Chicken and fish dishes for the non-vegetarian. A Sunday Jewish-style "all you can eat" brunch buffet (11 A.M.-3 P.M.) with blintzes, latkes, lox, and bagels. Open daily 11 A.M.-2 A.M.

Grappa ✪✪ *797 College Street, Tel. (416) 535 3337.* A romantic Italian restaurant. Snack on a dish of black olives with fresh bread before your meal. The specials include *zuppa di pesce,* mixed grill, and a wonderful selection of pastas. Reservations recommended. Open for dinner only Tues-Sun 5-11 P.M.

Kit Kat Bar & Grill ✪✪ *297 King Street W., Tel. (416) 977 4461.* Cats and movie posters decorate this popular Italian restaurant, and there's an occasional celebrity seated at one of the tables. Down-home cooking and an inexpensive but respectable Italian wine list. Open 11:30 A.M.-12:30 A.M.; Sat 5 P.M.-midnight; closed Sundays.

Lee Garden ✪ *331 Spadina Avenue, Tel. (416) 593 9524.* Chinese restaurant that specializes in seafood: fresh oysters, abalone, shrimp and pineapple, and steamed cod with black-bean sauce. Excellent and cheap. No reservations. Open daily 4 P.M.-midnight.

Mövenpick Marché ✪ *On the galleria of BCE Place, Front Street W., Tel. (416) 366 8986.* A large, noisy market where you pick up a ticket at the entrance and choose from a variety of trolleys, stands, and carts. Everything is cooked fresh on the spot, including fish and meat. They even have a *boccalino* to choose a glass of wine that will accompany your meal. No reservations. Open daily from 7:30 A.M.-2 A.M.

Masa ✪✪ *205 Richmond Street W., Tel. (416) 977 9519.* One of the best Japanese restaurants in Toronto, with sushi bar and fixed-price specials. Reservations recommended. Open for lunch Mon-Fri noon-2:30 P.M.; for dinner Mon-Sat 5-11 P.M., Sun 5-10 P.M.

Mercer Street Grill ✪✪-✪✪✪ *36 Mercer Street, Tel. (416) 599 3399.* Fusion cuisine, a combination of Asian and Western, makes for interesting dining. Try the steamed swordfish with tomato curry and Napa greens or the beef teriyaki with crimini mushrooms. Their desserts are equally unique—lemon treasure box filled with lemon *brûlée,* and chocolate sushi. They offer a Japanese garden for summer dining. Open daily 5-11 P.M.

Mildred Pierce ✪✪ *99 Sudbury Street, Tel. (416) 588 5695.* Like sitting inside an old movie set (and actually located in the back of Studio 99), Mildred Pierce offers a wonderful view of the city and an outdoor terrace. The food is equally enjoyable, with daily specials such as loin of pork with cabernet-cassis sauce and chutney, with rhubarb-meringue tartlet for dessert. Special brunch menu on Sundays (10 A.M.-3 P.M.). No reservations. Open Mon-Fri noon-2 P.M.; Sun-Thurs 6-10 P.M.; Fri-Sat 6-11 P.M.

N'Awlins ✪✪ *299 King Street W., Tel. (416) 595 1958.* An interesting combination of Italian and Cajun cuisines set to a backdrop of live jazz. Try the Cajun calamari. Reservations recommended. Mon-Fri 11 A.M.-11 P.M.; Sat 5 P.M.-1 A.M.; Sun 5 P.M.-midnight.

Palavrion ✪✪ *270 Front Street W., Tel. (416) 979 0060.* Continental food served in the most spectacular restaurant stage sets in Toronto (originally built to recreate Mövenpick Marché). It seats 380 people and has become a popular tourist spot due to the striking decor and the reasonable food. Open Sun-Thurs 11:30 A.M.-11 P.M.; Fri-Sat 11:30 A.M.-1 A.M.

Red Tomato ✪✪ *321 King Street W., Tel. (416) 971 6626.* Very popular bar/restaurant that draws a young crowd with video screens and wild decor. The food is Canadian eclectic, such as jalapeño linguine with chicken; or try their speciality, hot rocks cuisine (grilling on a granite rock). Open Mon-Fri 11:30 A.M.-12:30 A.M.; Sat noon-1 A.M.; Sun 4:30-10:30 P.M.

Taro Grill ✪✪ *492 Queen Street W., Tel. (416) 504 1320.* Very hip spot in Toronto with pastas and pizzas, braised rack of lamb or chicken dijonnaise. Reservations recommended. Open for lunch daily noon-4 P.M.; for dinner Sun-Thurs 6-11 P.M., Fri-Sat 6 P.M.-midnight.

Vanipha ✪ *193 Augusta Avenue, Tel. (416) 340 0491.* An example of Toronto's new cuisines, this Laotian/Thai restaurant serves fabulous Southeast-Asian food. They offer an assortment of curries and use authentic ingredients such as Thai basil, pandan leaves, and sticky rice. Open Mon-Sat noon-11 P.M.

Xango ✪✪ *106 John Street, Tel. (416) 593 4407.* New to Toronto, Latin cuisine is becoming trendy, and Xango is the best example of a fine Latin restaurant. Beautifully presented dishes and drinks, with an outdoor balcony and an ornately tiled floor —it's like walking into another world. Many different Latin cuisines are combined here, with unique style, such as their *empañada cebolla* (filled with onions, pears, blue cheese, and walnut vinaigrette). Open Mon-Sat 5-11 P.M.

DOWNTOWN EAST

Biaglo ✪✪✪ *155 King Street E., Tel. (416) 366 4040.* Biaglo's appeal is partially due to its magnificent courtyard and well-designed dining room. You do not feel crowded here, because of the large tables set far apart from each other and the high ceiling. It certainly helps that the Italian cuisine is the best in the city. Specials include such dishes as lasagna with salmon, scallops and shrimp, and veal chop with a wine and sage sauce. Reservations recommended. Open for lunch Mon-Fri noon-2:30 P.M.; dinner Mon-Sat 6-10:30 P.M.

Montréal Bistro and Jazz Club ✪✪ *65 Shelbourne Street, Tel. (416) 363 0179.* Toronto's Québecois restaurant with specialities like pea soup and *tourtière* (meat pie). Reasonably priced. There is a club attached to the restaurant where you'll find the best jazz in Toronto. Reservations recommended. Lunch Mon-Fri 11:30 A.M.-3 P.M.; dinner Mon-Thurs 6-11 P.M., Fri-Sat 6 P.M.-midnight.

Nami Japanese Seafood ✪✪✪ *55 Adelaide Street E., Tel. (416) 362 7373.* Very chic sushi and sashimi restaurant. Specializes in beef sashimi—thinly sliced beef with a *ponzu* sauce. Reservations recommended. Open for lunch Mon-Fri noon-2:30 P.M.; for dinner Mon-Sat 6-10:30 P.M.

Le Papillon ✪ *16 Church Street, Tel. (416) 363 0838.* An ever-popular fixture in Toronto, Le Papillon has a Mediterranean atmosphere. Although known for the crepes, their Canadian fare—onion soup, *tourtière* (meat pie), and *cretons* (pork pâté)—is superb. Added attractions are the many skylights that open up the dining room, and the wood-burning fireplace. Reservations recommended. Open for lunch Tues-Fri noon-2:30 P.M.; dinner Tues-Wed 5-10

P.M., Thurs 5-11 P.M., Fri 5 P.M.-midnight, Sat 10 A.M.-midnight, Sun (brunch) 10 A.M.-10 P.M.

Rodney's Oyster House ☺☺ *209 Adelaide Street E., Tel. (416) 363 8105.* The best oysters in the city, at a fun, crowded bar. The delicious chowder is a speciality of the house. Open Mon-Sat 11:30 A.M.-midnight.

The Senator ☺☺☺ *249 and 253 Victoria Street, Tel. (416) 364 7517.* This '40s-style diner offers full breakfast or a homestyle lunch consisting of meatloaf, burgers, or macaroni and cheese. In the dining-room section, the atmosphere becomes more elegant, with enclosed velvet booths and mahogany woodwork. The main attractions are the steaks and chops, and the jazz cabaret on the top floor. Diner open Mon-Fri 7:30 A.M.-8:30 P.M., Sat-Sun 8 A.M.-3 P.M.; steak house open Tues-Thurs 5-11:30 P.M., Fri-Sat 5-11:30 P.M., Sun 5-10 P.M.

Shopsy's ☺ *33 Yonge Street, Tel. (416) 365 3333.* This establishment has moved since its opening in 1925, but it remains the best deli in Toronto. They offer a great breakfast, too. Open Mon-Wed 7 A.M.-11 P.M., Thurs-Fri 7 A.M.-midnight, Sat 8 A.M.-midnight, Sun 8 A.M.-11 P.M.

Young Thailand ☺ *81 Church Street, Tel. (416) 368 1368.* Great Thai restaurant specializing in seafood dishes like sweet-and-sour fish and spicy shrimp at affordable prices. Look for their two other locations at 111 Gerrard Street E. and 165 John Street. Open Mon-Fri 11:30 A.M.-2 P.M.; daily 4:30-11 P.M.

MIDTOWN

Annapurna Vegetarian Restaurant ☺ *1085 Bathurst Street, Tel. (416) 537 8513.* Very quiet and filled with plants. Cuisine is Indian-based, plus salads and sandwiches. Nothing over C$6.50. Open daily from 11:30 A.M.-9 P.M. (except Wed until 6 P.M.)

Messis ✪✪ *97 Harbord Street, Tel. (416) 920 2186.* Mediterranean cuisine with a casual atmosphere. Delicious *tapenade*, polenta, and fish dishes. Covered patio. Open Tues-Fri noon-2 P.M., Sun-Thurs 5:30-10 P.M., Fri-Sat 5:30-11 P.M.

Mövenpick Bistretto ✪-✪✪ *133 Yorkville Avenue, Tel. (416) 926 9545.* Another popular spot with the locals, offering continental cuisine at reasonable prices. Shellfish and good atmosphere are the specialities. Open Tues-Sat 7:30 A.M.-2 A.M., Sun-Mon 7:30 A.M.-1 A.M.

Myth ✪✪ *417 Danforth Avenue, Tel. (416) 461 8383.* Like being in Classical Greece. Enjoy both the decor (Greek movies shown on TVs) and the food (Greek/Italian)—lemongrass mussels and pizzas. Open Mon-Thurs noon-2 A.M., Fri noon-4 A.M., Sat 1 P.M.-4 A.M., Sun 1 P.M.-2 A.M.

Ouzeri ✪ *500A Danforth Avenue, Tel. (416) 778 0500.* Located on Greek Row (the East End), this is the most popular Greek restaurant due to its large selection of beer and wine, its cheap prices, and its authentic food. No reservations. Open daily 11:30-2 A.M.

Southern Accent ✪✪ *595 Markham Street, Tel. (416) 536 3211.* Cajun cuisine. Three different dining rooms including patio. Save room for the bread pudding with bourbon sauce. Reservations recommended. Open daily 5:30-11 P.M.

Truffles ✪✪✪✪ *21 Avenue Road (in the Four Seasons Hotel), Tel. (416) 964 0411.* Truffles is in one of the best hotels in Toronto (see page 134). Excellent Provençal dining with some unique additions—salmon with fricassee and carrot-cumin sauce, or pan-seared duck with shiitake mushrooms and potato cannelloni. Be prepared to pay high prices for the excellence. Reservations recommended. Open Mon-Sat 6-11 P.M.

ABOUT BERLITZ

In 1878 Professor Maximilian Berlitz had a revolutionary idea about making language learning accessible and enjoyable. One hundred and twenty years later these same principles are still successfully at work.

For language instruction, translation and interpretation services, cross-cultural training, study abroad programs, and an array of publishing products and additional services, visit any one of our more than 350 Berlitz Centers in over 40 countries.

Please consult your local telephone directory for the Berlitz Center nearest you or visit our web site at http://www.berlitz.com.

Helping the World Communicate